The Beginning Teacher's
FIELD GUIDE

Embarking on Your
First Years

Tina H. Boogren

Solution Tree | Press

a division of
Solution Tree

555 North Morton Street
Bloomington, IN 47404
800.733.6786 (toll free) / 812.336.7700
FAX: 812.336.7790

email: info@SolutionTree.com
SolutionTree.com

Visit **go.SolutionTree.com/instruction** to download the free reproducibles in this book.

Printed in the United States of America

Library of Congress Cataloging-in-Publication Data

Names: Boogren, Tina, author.
Title: The beginning teacher's field guide : embarking on your first years /
    Tina H. Boogren.
Description: Bloomington, IN : Solution Tree Press, 2018. | Includes
    bibliographical references and index.
Identifiers: LCCN 2017042942 | ISBN 9781945349560 (perfect bound : alk. paper)
Subjects: LCSH: First year teachers--Handbooks, manuals, etc. |
    Teaching--Handbooks, manuals, etc.
Classification: LCC LB2844.1.N4 B658 2018 | DDC 371.102--dc23 LC record available at https://lccn.loc.gov/2017042942

Solution Tree
Jeffrey C. Jones, CEO
Edmund M. Ackerman, President

Solution Tree Press
President and Publisher: Douglas M. Rife
Editorial Director: Sarah Payne-Mills
Art Director: Rian Anderson
Managing Production Editor: Kendra Slayton
Senior Production Editor: Tonya Maddox Cupp
Senior Editor: Amy Rubenstein
Copy Editor: Miranda Addonizio
Proofreader: Evie Madsen
Text and Cover Designer: Abigail Bowen

This book is dedicated to all the beginning teachers, especially Brienne and Alexa, who are just starting their own incredible journeys in classrooms (and on carts) all over the world. I am your biggest fan.

ACKNOWLEDGMENTS

I am so grateful that Douglas Rife picked up this book and cheered it on so quickly and with such enthusiasm.

Thank you, Amy Rubenstein, for encouraging me to share my true voice with the world and for helping me reshape my original manuscript into something that I'm so incredibly proud of.

A very special thanks to both Mark Gardner and Yeshua Pastina for their meticulous help with ensuring that these words will appeal to all readers and for reassuring me that my voice matters.

To my husband, who never complained when I had to reschedule date night in order to write.

Finally, thank you to my parents, for always sneaking my books from their original shelves to the bestsellers table at the local bookstore.

Solution Tree Press would like to thank the following reviewers:

Kimberly Freeman
Latin Teacher
Lexington Middle School
Lexington, South Carolina

Claudia Kis
New Teacher Mentor
Woodburn School District
Woodburn, Oregon

Lindsay Frevert
Second-Grade Teacher
Van Derveer School
Somerville, New Jersey

Cheré Knotwell
New Teacher Mentor
Liberty Elementary School District #25
Buckeye, Arizona

Peggy Goddard
Training and Development Specialist
Howard-Suamico School District
Green Bay, Wisconsin

Karen Krantz
Sixth-Grade Teacher
Adams Elementary School
Spokane, Washington

Courtney Matulka
Science Teacher
Beadle Middle School
Omaha, Nebraska

Dora Miura
Geometry Teacher
Saipan Southern High School
Saipan, Northern Mariana Islands

Nardi Routten
Fourth-Grade Teacher
Frances K. Sweet Magnet School
Fort Pierce, Florida

Elizabeth Simons
Instructional Mentor
Greece Central School District
North Greece, New York

Jessica Tsoufiou
Fourth-Grade Teacher
Frazer Elementary School
Canton, Ohio

Lindi Wilson
Fifth-Grade Teacher
Princeton Alternative Elementary
  School
Birmingham, Alabama

Visit **go.SolutionTree.com/instruction** to download
the free reproducibles in this book.

TABLE OF CONTENTS

CHAPTER 3
The Disillusionment Phase 51

CHAPTER 4
The Rejuvenation Phase 69

APPENDIX B

ABOUT THE AUTHOR

Tina H. Boogren, PhD, is a former classroom teacher, English department chair, teacher mentor, instructional coach, professional developer, athletic coach, and building-level leader. She has presented at the school, district, state, and national levels and was a featured speaker at the International Literacy Association annual conference and Barnes & Noble's educators' nights.

Tina was a 2007 finalist for Colorado Teacher of the Year and received the Douglas County School District Outstanding Teacher Award eight years in a row, from 2002 to 2009. In addition to writing articles for the National Writing Project's *The Voice* and *The Quarterly*, she authored *In the First Few Years: Reflections of a Beginning Teacher* and *Supporting Beginning Teachers*. She coauthored *Motivating and Inspiring Students* and contributed to *Middle School Teaching: A Guide to Methods and Resources* and *Becoming a Reflective Teacher*.

Tina holds a bachelor's degree from the University of Iowa, a master's degree with an administrative endorsement from the University of Colorado Denver, and a doctorate from the University of Denver in educational administration and policy studies.

To learn more about Tina's work, visit www.facebook.com/selfcareforeducators or follow @THBoogren on Twitter and Instagram.

To book Tina H. Boogren for professional development, contact pd@SolutionTree.com.

First Things First

Welcome. I am so glad you are here. Our entire K–12 system needs you. Are you ready? (Say *yes*—because you are.)

Picture this: you and I are sitting down, across from each other, in a cozy coffee shop. See us leaning in toward one another. Allow me to introduce myself so that you and I start to build a relationship together, through these pages.

I'm Tina. I've been an educator my entire life, starting with reading to my stuffed animals and assigning homework to my imaginary students in my basement in Cedar Rapids, Iowa. Later I taught tennis lessons, became a summer day camp counselor, and mentored students during my undergraduate years at the University of Iowa, until I finally got my own classroom teaching middle school students outside of Denver, Colorado. That first year, in 1998, was rough. I almost didn't make it. I was so overwhelmed with attendance slips and grading and planning for four preps that I hit the (imaginary) wall—head-on—in October, just weeks after starting the school year. I have such a clear and precise memory of walking down the long hallway of my school, toward the front door, determined to take myself back to the mall to see if I could get my old job back because I was convinced that I simply wasn't cut out for this profession. It was Mary Dee Seibold who stepped out of her office and saved me that day. She picked me up as I was falling apart, put me back together, and is the sole reason that I'm still here. And now it's time for me to return the favor and reach out a hand to help *you*.

Since 1998, my career has shifted from classroom teacher to new teacher mentor to instructional coach to administrator and educational consultant and author. I have worked with thousands of educators and am proud to still call myself a teacher above all else. Even as I've transitioned from one role to another, my heart has always been with you, the beginning teacher, first and foremost. Because I remember. I see you. I recognize you. I hear you. And I'm here to help. It is my sincere honor and pleasure to assist you on this incredible journey.

Now read the following questions and imagine me asking them of you. I encourage you to pause and really think about them, and to then record your thoughts in the space provided. Your answers can be helpful as you embark.

Who or what inspires you and why?

_____

_____

_____

_____

_____

What was school like for you? What would you like to change about your own childhood experience and young adult experience in school?

_____

_____

_____

_____

_____

How do you learn best? How does your best friend
learn best? Why is it important to recognize that we
learn differently?

_____

_____

_____

_____

_____

Why did you choose this noble profession above all the
other careers available to you?

_____

_____

_____

_____

_____

What is your greatest hope for your first year? Your
fifth year? Your twenty-fifth year?

_____

_____

_____

_____

_____

What fuels you? In other words, what gives you energy?

_____

_____

_____

_____

_____

What does self-care look like for you?

_____

_____

_____

_____

_____

Your answers will become your own personal foundation on which to stand. As you experience the highest of highs and the lowest of lows these first years, I'll ask you to recall your answers to these questions and provide you with some new things to consider that relate to them. That way, you never forget how you got here. Because one day, *here* might look like an overcrowded classroom with papers piling up for you to grade, email messages requiring your responses, and empty candy bar wrappers overtaking your desk, while you fight back tears and wonder how to even take your next breath. But on another day, *here* might look like an energized classroom with students so fully engaged in purposeful small groups that they don't realize the bell is going to ring any minute. You'll experience both of these days and every iteration in between. How do I know? Because I've been in your shoes. I remember. Your answers to my questions will help ground and stabilize you as you move through all of your experiences during your first years.

As you embark on this journey, hopefully you'll have colleagues, mentors, instructional coaches, and administrators who will help you along the way, thoughtfully and with care. If you'd like one, professional mentor Michael Hyatt (n.d.) offers this advice for finding a mentor:

> If you have one in mind, start by building
> the relationship—just like you would anyone
> else. Don't lead with "Will you be my men-
> tor?" (That's like asking someone to marry
> you on the first date.) Instead, get to know

them. Look for opportunities to be generous.
Start small and see where it goes.

Whether you do or you don't, I want to tag along. I want to share with you what I've learned over the years about implementing essential research-based classroom strategies that positively impact student achievement from day one.

But here's what I know for sure: we can't stop there. Roughly half of new teachers leave within the first five years (Allen, 2005; Haynes, 2014). In describing their first-year teaching experience, beginning teachers often rely on words like "*arduous, confusing, chaotic,* and *overwhelming,*" and almost every veteran teacher who I know uses these same words when reflecting on his or her first few years in the classroom (Public Education Network, 2003, p. 19). Author and professor of education Max van Manen (1995) says that "beginning teachers often seem to feel the tension or the poor fit between what they learned about teaching and what they discover is required in the practice of teaching" (p. 4). As they wrestle with everything from managing difficult workloads to finding a work-life balance and from handling classroom management issues to addressing students' effort (or lack thereof), in addition to assessment pressure and lack of resources, beginning teachers often feel that their schools do not provide adequate support structures (Anthony & Kane, 2008).

The Beginning Teacher's Journey

First, I want you to understand how your first years in the classroom differ from the experiences of veteran teachers. Ellen Moir (2011) identifies a series of specific challenges that you will most likely encounter during your initial years of teaching. While her original work was published many years ago, these challenges still hold true. (Though they point specifically to the first year, they can occur during the first several. That's why I address beginning teachers, not just first-year teachers, in this book.) She organizes the challenges into five phases: (1) anticipation, (2) survival, (3) disillusionment, (4) rejuvenation, and (5) reflection, followed by a return to the anticipation phase at the end of your first year. Figure I.1 (page 6) depicts the typical progression of these phases during your first years on the job.

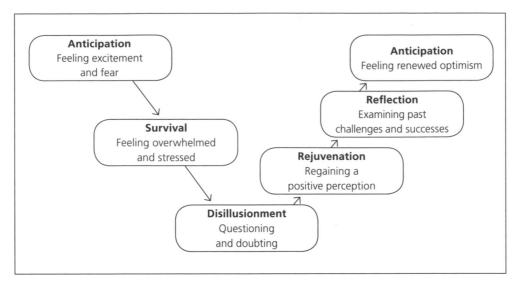

Source: Adapted from Moir, 2011.

Figure I.1: The phases of a first-year teacher's attitude toward teaching.

Of course, not every beginning teacher progresses through these phases exactly in this way, but having an understanding of them can help you move through the school year with more awareness, grace, and purpose. Allow me to briefly describe each phase here, knowing that I'll go into greater depth in the following chapters.

During the first anticipation phase, you are excited about the upcoming school year. You look forward to having your own classroom and the chance to make a difference in your students' lives. Your concerns during this phase may including setting up your classroom, locating curriculum materials, establishing rules and procedures, and building relationships with your colleagues, school leaders, parents, and students.

During the survival phase, you begin to realize sometimes harsh realities as requirements and expectations begin taking over the day, leaving you little time for planning or reflection. You are simply trying to stay afloat. Even in the face of these challenges and difficulties, most of you will work hard to maintain your energy and dedication, though you may find yourself falling short in some areas—typically your own self-care (less sleep and exercise as well as diminished connections with friends and family). This phase often occurs around the second to third month of school.

Hitting the wall may happen during the disillusionment phase. (It did for me.) Here, you may begin to question your own abilities and self-worth, and perhaps fall ill from stress (or wonder if your old job at Gap is still available). This phase often presents the greatest challenge for beginning teachers and typically falls between November and January. It is important for you to focus on self-care during this time and to recognize that what you're feeling is normal, even though these feelings are difficult. Know that this phase will not last forever and that by recognizing its challenges and supporting yourself, you will make it through.

The next phase—rejuvenation—often arrives shortly after winter break, once you have had the chance to reconnect and rest over the holiday break. Having a bit of time away can give you a new outlook and a renewed sense of your accomplishments. While in this phase, you begin feeling more hopeful and can begin focusing on your students' academic performances and your own teaching competence in ways that you couldn't when you were struggling through disillusionment. This beautiful rejuvenation phase can last into the spring.

Some veteran and beginning teachers I work with propose the existence of a second dip, associated with state testing, in the spring. This second dip might not drop as low as the initial disillusionment phase, but it's something to prepare for nonetheless. The second dip may also result from the long stretch that typically occurs between spring break and the end of the school year. As spring fever hits, this time can be especially challenging in the classroom for both you and your students.

Finally, as the school year comes to a close, you will most likely enter the reflection phase. Here, you begin looking back on all you have learned throughout the year, taking stock of which ideas and strategies worked best and which you'd like to change next year. At the end of the year, you may also feel powerful emotions tied to saying goodbye to your first groups of students. (You'll be glad you have photographs to remember them by.)

Eventually, you will enter a second anticipation phase. During this time, you will catch your breath and begin thinking ahead to the next year. The second anticipation phase usually occurs during summer break, when you have more time to reflect, plan, and re-energize.

Again, each beginning teacher will have his or her own upswings and dips and may not follow this pattern. You may hit the disillusionment phase earlier in the year, as I did, or you may not hit that phase at all. Conversely, you may cycle through many phases rather than experiencing just one in a single year. It's all normal. I promise.

And while beginning teachers feel each of these phases more profoundly than those with more experience, I'm here to tell you that this cycle isn't unique to your first year or years. Most veteran teachers will admit that they, too, experience these dips and upswings, even after many years in the classroom. Take comfort in this. You're not alone in your feelings. Additionally, it is important to know that there is no right or wrong way to experience your first years of teaching. What's important is understanding that feeling these dips and upswings is normal—no matter when or how they occur.

How to Use This Book

Ideally, this book is a resource for you—a K–12 beginning teacher—to use on your own, especially if you don't have a formal mentor. A school or district might also utilize this book as a book study for all new teachers to work through together. Finally, if your school pairs new teachers with formal mentors or coaches, they can use this book in conjunction with my book *Supporting Beginning Teachers* (Boogren, 2015) for mentors.

I organized this book chronologically, taking you through each phase in Moir's (2011) given order. As a beginning teacher, however, you may feel overwhelmed and intimidated by the sheer volume of instructional resources, strategies, and materials available to you through your school, district, and online. Knowing this, and based on my own experiences working with beginning teachers, I've deliberately selected the classroom strategies that I believe are the *most* essential for you to focus on during each phase of your first years in the classroom. I present those strategies to you in a concise and easily manageable manner, combined with a unique focus on reflection and self-care. Because of time constraints as a beginning teacher, you may decide not to read this book all at once. Instead, you might move from chapter to chapter or section to section as you're ready.

Table I.1 outlines the essential classroom strategies and self-care practices for each phase. The table serves as a preview to and an outline for the upcoming chapters.

Table I.1: Beginning Teacher Phases—Strategies and Practices

Phase	Classroom Strategies	Self-Care Practices
Anticipation	• Organizing your classroom's physical layout • Establishing rules and procedures • Understanding students' interests and backgrounds	• Getting adequate sleep • Eating a healthy diet • Exercising regularly
Survival	• Focusing on classroom management • Displaying objectivity and control • Noticing when students are not engaged	• Practicing mindfulness • Focusing on relationships
Disillusionment	• Developing relationships with all students • Celebrating students' successes • Focusing on positive student behaviors	• Practicing gratitude • Practicing kindness • Appreciating humor
Rejuvenation	• Demonstrating intensity and enthusiasm • Utilizing physical movement • Presenting unusual or intriguing information • Maintaining a lively pace	• Developing a growth mindset • Picturing your best possible future self
Reflection	• Employing questioning strategies • Asking all students in-depth questions • Demonstrating value and respect for all learners	• Being inspired • Writing yourself permission slips • Setting aside time to reflect • Reflecting with someone else
Second Anticipation	• Deciding how to arrange your classroom for next year • Creating things like charts, game templates, and posters	• Having fun • Acting like a kid again

One chapter is dedicated to each phase. Each chapter begins with a personal essay that I wrote during my own first few years in the classroom. In my essays, some of which first appeared in my book *In the First Few Years: Reflections of a Beginning Teacher* (Humphrey, 2003), I share insights in hopes of helping you feel less isolated. Then I ask you to consider some thoughts before getting into the actual strategies and practices. These prompts will help you understand how each phase is playing out for you personally.

Next, I provide the specific classroom strategies and self-care practices to focus on during this particular phase. Throughout, I'll invite you to visit **go.SolutionTree.com/instruction** for free reproducible versions of the prompts and reflections, as well as live links to additional resources. It is both well documented and common knowledge that the most important factor in student achievement is the teacher—not the curriculum, or subject-matter knowledge, or the standardized test, or the technology resources available but the actual teacher in the classroom (Hanushek, Kain, & Rivkin, 1998; McCaffrey, Lockwood, Koretz, & Hamilton, 2003; Rowan, Correnti, & Miller, 2002; Sanders, Wright, & Horn, 1997). Therefore, having the pedagogical skills to increase student achievement starting in these, your first years in the classroom, is essential. Classroom strategies will increase your expertise and significantly impact student achievement. While all the strategies are important and work any time of year, I've carefully prioritized them to correlate with the phases.

The self-care practices help prevent you from losing yourself in the midst of all these new demands. Many situations at this point in your life—even positive ones, such as a new job—lead to stress. Overwork also leads to stress, which makes us more prone to illness (Salleh, 2008). That, in turn, raises teacher absenteeism. More frequent teacher absences lead to lower student achievement (Miller, Murnane, & Willett, 2007). To compound these issues, research indicates that "many beginning teachers are reluctant to reveal problems or ask for help, believing that good teachers work things out for themselves" (Feiman-Nemser, 2010, p. 1033). That can lead to feelings of isolation, despair, and disillusionment, which in turn "are associated with high levels of stress [and] depression" (Southwick & Charney, 2012, p. 108). This reality highlights the importance of self-care for beginning teachers. Many authors who write books designed for you over-look such practices or view them as afterthoughts. I take a firm stand that self-care practices are *as essential* as the classroom strategies because if you are not your best self, you will not be sturdy enough to face the challenges that appear during your first few years in the classroom. You can easily incorporate these suggestions into your schedule. I do not want it to feel as if you're just adding to your already overflowing to-do list. I will offer gentle reminders and daily habits that can help you feel more stable during this often turbulent time.

To increase your impact on student achievement, you must be a reflective practitioner. Reflection is an essential part of developing expertise and increasing one's pedagogical skills. As you come into your own as a professional educator, it is imperative that you reflect on what's working, what's not working, and why—for both you and your students. Research supports this as well:

> Reflection, as a thoughtful and a caring act, goes to the heart of the instructional relationship. It is not only a tool of skilled practice, but also a feeling that helps educators to teach effectively and intelligently rather than unthinkingly, dogmatically or prejudicially. (Roskos, Vukelich, & Risko, 2001, p. 617)

Finally, in each chapter I provide you with reflection questions relating to both the classroom strategies as well as the self-care practices presented there. To make reflection as easy as possible, I've included space at the end of each chapter and in the margins where you can record your thoughts so you don't have to keep track of a separate notebook or journal. By using this book *as* your journal, you'll have the strategies and your reflections all in one place. That being said, you know yourself better than anyone else. Do what works for you—use a separate notebook, type your notes in a Google Doc, or make an audio recording. The medium doesn't matter. What matters is that you have a place to record your thoughts. You may choose to share some of your reflections with a mentor or coach, or you might keep them to yourself; again, it's up to you. The important part is pausing, checking in, and recording your current observations and feelings so that you can actually *see* yourself grow, change your perspective, and improve—alongside your inevitable frustrations and setbacks.

You may focus on what is *not* going well when you reflect, but it is important to acknowledge and reflect on successes as well. Kendyll Stansbury and Joy Zimmerman (2000) point out, "Recognizing and understanding their successes not only provides an enormous boost in confidence, but helps beginning teachers build on those strengths" (p. 9). Like the balance between the professional and personal, I encourage you to focus on what is going well along with areas for growth and improvement. Reflection questions remind you of this during each phase.

In addition to prompts throughout the book, I encourage you to record anything else that you want to remember. Consider picking up a glue stick while you're at the store so you can paste in notes from students, parents, administrators, or colleagues, current events that occurred during the year, photographs of your first classroom, your first students, your first holiday gift, your first confiscated note between students, and the like. (You can glue those mementos to the pages in appendix B, on page 119, of this book so you've got everything in one place.) If you are using a Google Doc or other online application, you could save notes there. Years from now, when you look back on your reflections, you will be humbled and astonished at how far you've come. You might even be ready to pay it forward and use your experiences to lend a hand to the next generation of beginning teachers.

Now take a deep breath.

You've got this; you've so got this.

CHAPTER 1

The Anticipation Phase

Congratulations! You got the job! Right now, you are primed and ready to embark on your new career as an educator. You are ready to save the world and may be thinking about how to set up your classroom or drooling over new school supplies. Welcome to the anticipation phase. While here, you may recognize butterflies in your stomach. You are likely overcome by a wide range of emotions—everything from hope and excitement to wonder and nervousness—as you prepare to meet and build quality relationships with your first students. You may arrange and rearrange desks and supplies as well as locate curricula and materials during this phase. It is likely you'll spend the first few weeks focused on meeting and getting to know new colleagues, school leaders, parents, and your students. The first day of school is an especially exciting time in your career; there will never be another like this one.

I wrote the following essay after my own first few years teaching. It may provide some additional validation and support for you during the anticipation phase.

The First Week of School

About a week or so before the school year, you'll start having dreams (or nightmares) about the year's impending start. In them, you'll be naked at the front of the room, or the students will be three-headed monsters that never stop chirping. This is to be expected. Don't put too much pressure on getting quality sleep the night before school starts. Peaceful dreams probably aren't going to happen. Watch some good comedy movies and vow to get that beautiful, deep, restful sleep after the first week of school.

Prior to your first day with students, you will be at school for three or four days meeting veteran teachers, trying to set up your classroom (which you'll rearrange a million times and still never like), getting curriculum thrown at you, and playing embarrassing get-to-know-you games with staff. This is administration's attempt to make you feel more confident, but most likely it won't help. Instead, consider this time where you're building relationships with your colleagues. You'll wake up in the morning, put on your well-considered first-day outfit, and drive to school with bigger butterflies flapping in your stomach than you had on your first day of school as a student. Your palms will sweat. When you arrive, you'll immediately want to rearrange your room—again. And you'll look through the class list (which you received just this morning) and panic because you can't pronounce a single name on it.

Please remember that your students are nervous, too. They may not admit it or show it, depending on their age, but they are. Take it easy today. You won't be able to do everything that you plan on getting done, so accept that and spend the day shaking your students' hands, attempting to pronounce their names, and easing everyone's tensions. I wouldn't even begin to get into curriculum or expectations at this point. You and your students have too many other things on your minds, so consider any information given out today lost by the time your students leave your room. This is when I like to play a game like the one in which we write down two truths and one lie about ourselves on a note card, and the class tries to guess which one of the statements is the lie. Any of these get-to-know-you games are good, low-stress ways to ease your fears on this first day and will immediately start setting up the comfortable, inviting environment that you're hoping for and will help you remember students' names.

The entire first week will probably be a mess. The schedule will change three times as the administration holds schoolwide assemblies focusing on the code of conduct. Students will leave and enter and leave your class as schedules are rearranged and changed again. More than once with your class you'll have to go over the supply list, expectations, and money that's due. Instead of getting frustrated that you haven't yet gotten to the content, try to relax and use this time to really get to know your students. You'll get to the content eventually. Everyone in the school has to go over the same things. Mr. Kline next door is not already doing science experiments while you're still collecting dues.

This first-week chaos has nothing to do with being a new teacher. This will happen every year. You might believe that by your fourth year you'll be able to whip through all the preliminaries in two days, but it won't happen. Your students need all that information (as tedious as it may be), so accept it, go over it with them, and play when you can. Shake their hands at the door, ask them one interesting question, and make it your top priority to know their names within one week of school. It's not easy for those of you with lots of students, but it's so important. They deserve for you to know their names (and to pronounce them correctly).

You'll go home each night this first week (after the sun sets) exhausted. Make and freeze meals or plan for take-out food before the school year starts. You may want to let friends and family know, ahead of time, that you will be unavailable this week and that you'll call them on Friday after your three-hour nap. Find your favorite method of releasing stress and use it this week. Maybe you need to go sweat at the gym for an hour, or maybe you need to fill the bathtub with bubbles and crawl in with a good book. Whatever your stress reliever is, do it—especially this week. But also make it a habit for the entire year. Remember to take care of yourself.

Try not to scold yourself for things that go wrong. Talk to yourself as you would talk to your students—gently and kindly and with forgiveness. As you drive home from school, sit in the bathtub, or run on the treadmill, congratulate yourself on doing this job. Name three specific things that you did well today and applaud yourself. If you remembered that student Tracy likes turtles, pat yourself on the back. When you do something well, smile and record your accomplishment so you can look back on it later.

Prompts

As you learn about strategies and practices in this chapter, consider the following questions.

What words do I hope students will use to describe me after meeting me for the first time?

How can I ensure that the first day is a success? What about the first week? The first month?

How will I celebrate my successes?

Classroom Strategies

Before we dig into the classroom strategies that I suggest focusing on during the anticipation phase, let me clarify the difference between regular practice and deliberate practice. *Regular practice* is a skill that has become automatic. On the other hand, *deliberate practice* involves a concentrated effort (Colvin, 2008; Ericcson, 2006). Let's use driving as an example because at one time or another, it requires both kinds of practice. *Learning* how to drive requires concentrated effort—deliberate practice. You may have learned in an empty parking lot, with the radio turned off and both hands on the wheel. Eventually, with enough repetition, driving becomes automatic and, rather than requiring deliberate practice, is regular practice. Too much automaticity can lead us to believe that we can engage in other activities while driving—texting, talking on the phone, or even shaving legs (which truly I have seen). The key is learning how to stay engaged even though the skills have become automatic in many ways. The same is true in your classroom.

As you get started teaching, nearly every skill requires deliberate practice. Before routines and procedures become automatic, you may need to engage in concentrated effort with nearly every strategy involved with teaching. Eventually, you will be able to deliver routines, procedures, and other strategies with automaticity and therefore with less effort. When you reach automaticity on certain skills and strategies, you can focus deliberate practice efforts on other areas, like teaching content, engaging students, and reflecting. Staying engaged even after many skills have become automatic ensures that you're meeting your learners' needs.

To begin, let's think about which classroom strategies will benefit you most right now: organizing your classroom's physical layout, establishing rules and procedures, and understanding students' interests and backgrounds.

Organizing Your Classroom's Physical Layout

Your classroom will be your second home for the next year. As you begin transforming the physical space into one that welcomes and supports learning, it can be helpful to understand the core characteristics that a classroom should embody. In other words, you'll want to ensure that your classroom is safe, functional, welcoming, and warm for all your students (Marzano, 2007, 2017).

How can you create a safe, functional space? First, ensure that students have the space to safely move around the room. Functionality requires that your students easily see you wherever you're teaching in the room and have access to equipment and materials. Depending on your classroom and teaching style, you might cluster students in small groups or use rows. It's often easier to start the year in alphabetical rows because it minimizes talking, facilitates quick attendance taking, and helps you learn students' names. As the year progresses, you can determine how students can move to pairs, triads, or groups of four from their original positions.

As you think about safety and functionality, consider asking yourself the following questions.

* How will I position the desks, furniture, technology, and supplies so that students can see the front of the room? Sit in every desk to confirm that each student can see the classroom's main focus and anywhere you might stand to teach. Walk between the desks to ensure that you can reach every desk within a few steps. This helps you address discipline concerns and use proximity to reach all students quickly and easily.

- How will I assign students to their seats? Alphabetical order by last name or first? How will students know where to sit when they enter my classroom for the very first time? (You can label the desks or tables with sticky notes, and you can display the seating chart on the SMART Board or whiteboard.)

- Where will I place my own desk?

- Are supplies easy to obtain and keep organized?

- Are my emergency procedures posted and easy to follow?

And how will you make your room warm and welcoming to students? Elementary *and* secondary students like entering a space that feels inviting. You can create this environment by being conscious of your wall space and bulletin boards. Consider leaving some white space so that you don't overwhelm students and so that you have room to add as the year progresses. Display information that will be useful for students: content standards, learning goals, essential questions, schedule, agenda, homework, and content-specific posters. Make it so the classroom feels like everyone's space, not just yours as the teacher. Post students' pictures along with their names and birthdays (this will also help you learn their names more quickly), school newsletter articles that highlight them, or their exemplary work. You may not have much personal information about your students at the beginning of the school year, so you can start with information about yourself instead. Students will be extremely excited to get to know you. (Well, elementary students will be extremely excited; secondary students may not show it quite as much but do know that they are excited deep down inside.) In this space, you could share pictures of you and your family, friends, or pet, postcards from your favorite places, or a word cloud that has adjectives describing you. (Visit Wordle at www.wordle.net to create one.)

Another warm welcome includes greeting your students at the door every single day, starting from day one. Shake their hands (or give a high five or a fist bump), make eye contact, and say their names as they enter your classroom. It is a simple way to connect with every student on a daily basis. This won't take too long. You don't need to have extended conversations.

As you think about how you can make your classroom both warm and welcoming, consider the following questions.

- What messages do my walls and bulletin boards convey?

- Where and how do I recognize and acknowledge students in my classroom?

- Would I want to be a student in my class? Why or why not?

If you're a beginning teacher who *doesn't* have a classroom, I see you, too. You may teach music or language and have to move from room to room with all your teaching materials. While moving from classroom to classroom (usually with a cart) certainly isn't ideal, it can be a rite of passage for many new teachers and you, too, will survive. Even if you don't have your own room, you can create an inviting space for your students. Your cart can make you smile, too.

- How will I share this physical space with others? Is there a place where I can leave materials, even if I'm using the room for just one period? How can I alter the space for my students? How can I respect the other teachers' needs? (Discuss these questions with the teachers with whom you're sharing space. Don't make any assumptions.)

- How can I make my cart inviting? Can I add a string of lights, a horn, or stickers? How can I own it?

- Am I staying organized? Can I store my supplies in smaller carts, crates, or bags for easier mobility? (Strict organization is essential when you're moving spaces throughout the day. Try blogger Angela Watson's website at https://thecornerstoneforteachers.com/teachers-ideas for shared organization ideas and The Oriental Trading Company at www.bit.ly/2zQToec for supplies; access live links to these and other websites at **go.SolutionTree.com/instruction**.)

Establishing Rules and Procedures

As a beginning teacher, you are probably feeling anxious about classroom management; this is a normal concern. You know that the classroom requires rules and procedures so students can learn. It is important to keep the list short and sweet. Between five and eight rules per class is a good guideline.

The Marzano Compendium of Instructional Strategies (Marzano Resources, n.d.) outlines a six-step process that may help you generate rules and procedures with your students:

1. Facilitate a whole-class discussion about the characteristics of a class that facilitates learning.

2. Assemble small groups of students and ask them to create initial lists of suggestions for rules. Provide examples of previous classes' rules if necessary.

3. Combine the rule suggestions from all the small groups into one list and post it somewhere in the classroom.

4. Facilitate another whole-class discussion about the aggregated list of rules. Groups who suggested a rule can explain why they think it is important, and students can discuss the benefits of each one.

5. Have the class vote on each rule and add the rules that obtain a majority (or consensus, depending on the teacher's preferences) to the class's final list of rules.

6. Facilitate a whole-class discussion about the final list of rules and address students' questions or concerns. Students might design procedures for rules that need further clarification. (p. 10)

You can also consider asking your students to monitor their behavior and modify the established expectations at various times throughout the year. For example, you could revisit the rules you established early in the year at each grading period to ensure they are still working for your class.

It may be helpful to tie rules and procedures to the classroom's physical layout. For example, if you want your classroom to feel like a community, you might ask students to connect with one another by saying hello to at least five students every single day. The following list provides further examples. The following rules are for the elementary level.

- Help at least one other student every day.
- Treat other people's property as you would like your property treated.
- Think before you speak.
- Keep your hands to yourself.

These rules are for the secondary level.

- Bring all necessary materials to class.
- Be in your assigned seat when the bell rings.
- Respect others and their property.
- Listen and participate equally and respectfully.

List your ideas here.

- _____
  _____

- _____
  _____

Establishing procedures for both yourself and your students can help enforce the established rules. It is essential that students engage with the procedures so that they build muscle memory around them and can do them automatically. Consider these sample procedures for the elementary level.

- Begin the day with specific administrative tasks: taking attendance and lunch counts, acknowledging birthdays, reviewing the schedule, and reciting the Pledge of Allegiance.

- End the day by tidying the room, reviewing homework or reminders, and putting away supplies and materials.

Consider these for the secondary level.

- Take attendance at the beginning of each class period while students are engaged in bell work (an activity they complete upon entering the classroom).

- Address students who missed work due to an absence and collect any homework or paperwork.

- Track students who are tardy.

- Review the homework with students at the end of each class period.

Additionally, it is important to have procedures for when students leave the classroom; respond to emergency procedures; use equipment, technology, and materials; move to group work; and engage in individual seatwork. Here are some suggestions, with space to record your own ideas.

- Design a pass or two for when students need to leave the classroom. Determine when students can use the pass (for instance, only when you aren't directly teaching) and how you will keep track of who is gone (such as sign-out sheets near where you keep the pass).

- Have a folder with all the necessary information for emergencies, including class lists and procedures for each emergency scenario (such as fire, tornado, and intruder). Your school should provide the information before the year begins. Keep this folder in a designated space.

- Determine how you will distribute, collect, and keep track of materials. For example, you can assign this job to students or distribute and collect materials yourself.

- Model how to move in and out of small groups as well as the behavior expectations within groups, including appropriate noise levels and individual responsibilities within groups.

- Provide seatwork expectations, including what to do when a student finishes early. Have worksheets or supplemental activities available.

- _____

  _____

- _____

  _____

Understanding Students' Interests and Backgrounds

Teaching is all about relationships. I simply cannot stress this enough. Without solid, effective relationships, no learning can take place. Additionally, classroom management problems typically stem from a breakdown in teacher-student relationships, and so it is imperative to build positive relationships with your students from the beginning of the year. Ignore outdated advice such as not to smile until Christmas, which does not create a supportive, caring environment or foster strong relationships. Smiling is essential to building positive relationships with students! Not smiling establishes hostility, not trust, and creates a difficult year. On the other hand, you are the authority, not your students' friend.

You can get to know your students by handing out a survey during the first few days of school. In it, you can ask questions about their background, interests, and goals. (A bonus is that, by providing a written survey, you'll get a glimpse into their writing abilities. If you teach primary-aged students, you might send the survey home and ask parents to transcribe their children's answers, or meet individually with students to ask them a few questions.)

The survey can include a variety of questions, including any and all of the following ideas. Visit **go.SolutionTree.com/instruction** for a free reproducible version of this survey.

- What are the three most important things that I should know about you?
- What would you like to know about me?
- What do you love about school? What don't you like about school?
- What are you proudest of?
- How do you learn best?
- What's your favorite thing to do when you're not in school?
- How would you spend a month of Saturdays?
- What would you do if you knew you couldn't fail?

Self-Care Practices

As we discussed earlier, self-care is a tool for surviving *and* thriving that teachers often overlook. Being aware of various methods means you can enter each new phase with tools that make the school day easier and mitigate burnout.

You will most likely feel energetic and excited during the anticipation phase, so use it to your advantage. It's important to establish the foundations and daily routines *now*, before you start to feel overwhelmed by the stress of the survival and disillusionment phases. These habits serve as the bedrock of survival for the remainder of the school year. In the following sections, I provide essential practices that hold the other self-care practices in place as the year progresses. The basics include getting adequate sleep, eating a healthy diet, and exercising regularly.

Getting Adequate Sleep

We all know the difference we feel in our day when we've had enough sleep versus when we're running on empty. Getting enough sleep is a key component to being the best teacher (and person) you can possibly be. The National Sleep Foundation (n.d.b) recommends that adults get between seven to nine hours of sleep each night. In fact, research shows that not getting enough sleep causes accidents because being tired can slow down your reaction time as much as when you're drunk. Additionally, lack of sleep impairs alertness, concentration, reasoning, and problem solving and can contribute to overeating and depression (Peri, n.d.). Not good.

While it may be tempting to stay up late working on lesson plans or grading papers, getting enough sleep is an absolute priority. And about electronics in the bedroom, the National Sleep Foundation (n.d.a) has this to say: "Careful studies have shown that even our small electronic devices emit sufficient light to miscue the brain and promote wakefulness," which means that it's essential to leave your phone in another room, shut it down for the night, or turn it off when you're ready for bed. (Ask for an old-school alarm clock for your birthday this year.)

To establish a sleep routine, consider the following suggestions from Ingrid Prueher (2017), a pediatric and adult sleep and nutrition consultant.

- Prepare for the next day. Decide what you'll wear, prepare your lunch, pack your bag, and so on. Try setting an alarm an hour before the time you'd like to go to bed. When it goes off you can listen to calming music, read, take a bath, and turn off electronics.

- Whatever you do to relax before bed (for example, reading or writing in your journal), do so in a softly lit room. Our biological clocks are set by the sun and the moon and so as soon as the sun goes down, the melatonin in our bodies starts to increase and this prepares our bodies for sleep ("Blue light," 2015).

- Avoid eating a large meal close to bedtime but try not to go to bed hungry. Have a small, healthy snack as needed.

- Keep your bedroom between sixty-eight and seventy-two degrees.

- If light wakes you easily, try using blackout shades or an eye pillow. If noise bothers you, try a white noise machine or phone app.

- If you decide to keep your phone in your bedroom, put it on Do Not Disturb or Airplane mode so alerts and reminders do not wake you up.

- Treat yourself to new or clean pillows, sheets, duvet covers, and mattress pads.

After establishing a solid sleep routine, do your best to stick with it, even on the weekends. Sleeping in late disrupts the balance between our sleep drive and circadian clock, which can result in disrupted sleep and make you cranky and groggy (Restonic, 2017).

Eating a Healthy Diet

I can't stress enough the importance of a healthy diet. The food that you put into your body directly impacts your mood, sleep habits, energy level, and outlook (Grothaus, 2015; Selhub, 2015). Maintaining a healthy diet can be a challenge for educators of all experience levels because they are often surrounded by unhealthy options. It can be difficult to say no, especially when you're feeling stressed or low on time or energy. Strive to eat mostly foods that come from plants (including vegetables, fruits, whole grains, and legumes) and try to limit highly processed foods as best you can (Pollan, as cited in DeNoon, 2009). I love the simplicity of Michael Pollan's advice: "Eat food. Not too much. Mostly plants" (2009). By doing so, you'll feel better and have more energy, both of which are keys to success in the classroom.

Also try to implement these keys to optimal wellness that Berkeley Wellness–University of California (n.d.) outlines.

- Pay attention to portion sizes.

- Get more whole grains.

- Limit refined grains and added sugar.

- Enjoy more fish and nuts.

- Cut down on animal fat.

- Avoid trans fats.

- Don't worry about cholesterol.

- Keep sodium down and potassium up.

- Get enough calcium and vitamin D.

- Choose whole foods over supplements.

- Be cautious with liquid calories. Drink water!

- Limit alcohol consumption.

Eat a healthy breakfast; pack a healthy lunch and snacks the night before. Allow yourself time to be fully present while you're eating by taking a few deep breaths before you begin and eating without distractions, if at all possible.

Exercising Regularly

Establishing and maintaining a regular exercise routine offers so many benefits. According to the Mayo Clinic (2016), all of the following are key benefits of regular physical activity.

- Health condition and disease resistance

- Improved mood

- Boosted energy

- Better sleep

Best of all, exercise can be fun. Try wearing an activity monitor and challenging yourself (and possibly your colleagues) to get at least ten thousand steps per day. My Fitbit is such a great motivator for me. I've been known to walk laps around my house just to meet my daily step goal, and I thrive on the challenges that I have with my fellow wearers. It's amazing how motivating it can be to "win."

Because you're moving nonstop during your workday, you're ahead of the game compared to those with more sedentary jobs. The U.S. Department of Health and Human Services Office of Disease Prevention and Health Promotion (n.d.) states, "All adults should avoid inactivity. Some physical activity is better than none, and adults who participate in any amount of physical activity gain some health benefits." Beyond that, for substantial health benefits, it suggests that adults do a minimum of 150 minutes a week of moderate intensity exercise (in which it's difficult to talk without being winded) or seventy-five minutes of vigorous intensity activity (where you can't speak because you're so winded). Do aerobic activity in episodes of at least ten minutes and spread it throughout the week.

That being said, even a small amount of exercise is a good thing. I've known teachers who have engaged in a challenge where they start with just a few push-ups and add a few more daily, until they're able to do one hundred push-ups without stopping. I've known other teachers who've participated in thirty days' worth of burpees, sit-ups, or squats. Each of these challenges takes fewer than five minutes per day. Tap into your competitive side if you have one. These challenges are easy to find online and help build camaraderie among staff members. The following ideas are small, manageable ways to stay active.

- Park as far away from the school as you can.
- Take the stairs rather than the elevator.
- Use a restroom that is farther away from your classroom.
- Go see someone you need to talk to rather than sending an email.
- Conduct a walking meeting when possible.
- Sit on a stability ball rather than a desk chair.
- Engage in active brain breaks with your students; see chapter 4, on page 73, for examples.
- Use your school's gym equipment: walk around the track, use the free weights, or shoot baskets at the end of the day.

You might even consider getting a group of colleagues together to walk or run in a local race or start a walking or running club that meets a few days a week before or after school. Schedule time in your calendar for exercise, just the way you would schedule a doctor's appointment.

Reflections

Set aside time each day to reflect. The following prompts, related to classroom strategies and self-care practices for this phase in your first year, encourage this reflection. You don't need to respond to all of these in one sitting. Instead, dig into one or two at a time. Use the space at the end of this chapter to write about any other concerns or celebrations that you notice during the anticipation phase.

Classroom Strategy Prompts

Consider the following prompts in light of the anticipation phase.

+ Can I easily move around my room? Are supplies easy to get to? Are there places where I trip or stumble? (Consider doing an audit every few weeks to ensure that your physical space is welcoming to your students and yourself. You spend a large part of your life here; make it beautiful and functional.)

+ How does the space make me feel when I enter in the morning? How does my classroom look, feel, sound, and taste? (Consider doing an audit of your classroom using your five senses. For example, do you have healthy snacks for yourself and for your students? Is your room clean? Can you use an essential oils diffuser or open a window for fresh air?)

+ Do the rules and procedures I have set feel kind? Do they establish the type of classroom community that I want? Can I easily recite my rules and procedures, which lets me know that I don't have too many? Are students responding well to my rules and procedures so far?

+ Do I know all of my students' names? Have I learned about each student's interests and background through conversations or a survey? How do I welcome students each day? Are there students

I need to learn more about (such as those who are more reserved or have a specific need or behavior that I need to understand better)? (Commit to reaching out to those students this week.)

◆ Have I celebrated the successes, no matter how small? (Every day, record one or two things that you're proud of. Perhaps you remembered to take attendance during the first ten minutes of class, or a student you've been struggling with smiled at you today.)

Self-Care Practice Prompts

Consider the following prompts in light of the anticipation phase.

◆ What is my sleep pattern? Am I getting enough sleep? If not, can I go to bed five minutes earlier each night this week? Am I having trouble turning off my thoughts? (Try journaling before bed so you can get those thoughts out of your mind before trying to sleep.)

◆ What have my food choices looked like lately? Is what I eat helping me thrive, or is it making me feel sluggish and bad? Am I drinking enough water? Am I often getting fast food on the way home? Am I mindlessly snacking on the treats that appear at meetings?

◆ What exercise or movement have I engaged in lately? How much am I moving throughout the day? Is it enough or would I like to add more? Can I find five minutes during my plan time, or before or after school, to take a lap around the building? If exercise has always been important to me, am I still prioritizing this need?

— NOTES —

CHAPTER 2

The Survival Phase

During the survival phase, which typically occurs around the second or third month of school, you begin to fully realize the sometimes harsh realities of a teacher's daily work and demands. You may have little time for planning or reflection and struggle to simply stay afloat. Maybe you're spending an incredible amount of time at school, feel like you have hardly any time for yourself, family, or friends, and your self-care practices are starting to slip. You might have your first cold of the year but not want to stay home and take care of yourself (or deal with planning for a substitute teacher). The papers might be stacking up on your desk and you might dread department, grade-level, or faculty meetings because you seem to get twenty new to-do items every time you attend one. You may be uncomfortable working with parents and, by this point in the year, you may be talking with them quite a bit. Do not despair. I am here to help!

I want to share the details of when I hit the wall during my own first year of teaching. I wrote this essay during the disillusionment phase (which is in chapter 3, on page 51), but I want to share it while you're in the throes of the survival phase. I'm hoping to keep you from walking blindly into the disillusionment phase—or at least make things feel less horrendous, starting here and now, during the survival phase.

Mentorships Are Invaluable

I am lucky enough to work in a school district that provides a building resource teacher. This person plans staff development and leads numerous committees, but most important, this person has the precious duty of mentoring new teachers. If I hadn't had a mentor during my first year, I would have left my classroom in October and never gone back. After weeks of meetings, creating lesson plans for my administration to review, and late nights grading papers, I finally—and fully—hit the wall. One day I sat at my desk during plan time, looking at the never-ending paper piles, and my heart began to beat much too quickly. I was tired and hungry, and I had a migraine-level headache. I had felt this way for the past two months. I could not take it anymore. My room was used for a health class and then a Spanish class during my plan time, and my patience ended as the students' volume continued rising. I aimlessly walked down the hallway looking for an escape. If I didn't find it by the time I hit the front door, I was going out and never coming back. This is when my mentor, Mary Dee, walked up and asked me if I was OK. My tears began to flow immediately with just this simple question.

Mary Dee pulled me into her office, shut the door, grabbed the Kleenex, and said, "Cry." I did. I didn't even say one word for a good five minutes as she rubbed my back and whispered, "I know." As I finally started to get myself together and explain that I didn't think I was cut out for twelve-hour days teaching, she just smiled at me and said again, "I know." I didn't understand. I felt like a failure. I was two months into my dream job and failing fast. I thought that I would be teacher of the year by this point. I thought that student teaching was the hard part and once I got my own classroom, I'd begin to get it. I thought that the first week would be the worst, but then things would begin falling into place. But here it was, October, and nothing was falling into place. Nothing. My lessons were failing, I still wasn't sure what IEP stood for, and I had forgotten to pay rent on time for the past two months.

Mary Dee spent the next hour explaining to me that I was normal—that this is what happens to nearly every new teacher.

This is why *she* had a job. She was the new teacher mentor *because* new teachers need support and lots of it. She helped me see that I was on the right track. My crying meant that I cared, and that's the number one requirement for a teacher. If I didn't care, then upon hitting the wall I would have simply stood up, walked out the front door, and checked the help wanted ads.

I liked what Mary Dee was saying, but I was still exhausted, overwhelmed, and scared. I was nodding politely, attempting to smile, and blowing my nose. She got up, retrieved my purse and coat (she left the papers and gradebook), hugged me, and sent me home. Her direct orders were to go to bed and not to come back tomorrow. She explained that I was no good to my students if I wasn't first good to myself and that having a substitute tomorrow would be OK. She pointed at me and said, "I know you, Tina. You'll try to show up here tomorrow and teach, and if you do, I'm going to just send you home, so you may as well save yourself the trip." I crawled to my car, to my apartment, to my bed, and slept until noon the following day.

Upon waking up, I made myself some coffee and began reprioritizing. I figured out what to do first, what could wait, and who to ask for help. For example, I knew I needed to carefully plan my immediate lessons but that preparing for the preconference meeting with my principal could wait and that asking my mentor for guidance here would help to ease my anxiety about what to expect. I had a better sense of direction and a fresh perspective. I had given myself time to breathe and felt ready to go back and try this teaching stuff again. One more time.

I did go back, and it was hard; the weeks after that were hard, too. The first years are just hard, period. I hit more walls, but that happened less as I got into a routine. As someone who thrives on a schedule, finding a workable routine was essential to my survival not only during my first few years but later years as well. I survived because I wanted to and because, more than anything else, Mary Dee hugged me and told me I was normal on that October afternoon.

Everyone needs a mentor. Hopefully your school or district provides one who is caring and supportive. If not, find one on your own. *Someone* in your school is worth going to when you need to cry or laugh or vent.

If there is no one, you may need to consider finding a mentor outside of your school or district. Yes, a mentor is *that* important. It's good to have a support system of friends and family members outside of school, too, but having someone who truly understands what you're going through and will help guide you is vital. This person can identify who to ask about the upcoming testing period, understands how overwhelming the school day can be, and doesn't feel put out by your questions or concerns. Receiving this guidance does not mean you're failing. Needing guidance and support is normal. Remember this in a few years when that new teacher is aimlessly walking toward the front door and repay the favor.

Prompts

As you learn about strategies and practices in this chapter, consider the following questions.

What does my support system look like at school?

What does my support system look like outside of school?

What type of support is most helpful to me? How can I ask for help when I need it?

Classroom Strategies

As you know, things can get difficult in this phase. These classroom strategies will help keep things running as smoothly as possible in your classroom. By focusing on classroom management, displaying objectivity and control, and noticing when students are not engaged, you can create a classroom in which you can identify and address problems before they get out of hand.

Focusing on Classroom Management

After establishing rules and procedures in your classroom (see chapter 1, on page 13), monitor how they're working. Do you need to make any adjustments? You can adjust rules and procedures any time, particularly if you notice that a certain one isn't working; you don't have to wait until the end of the quarter or next year or even next Monday. For example, if students in small groups are not paying attention while you're directly instructing at the beginning of class, you have every right to move the students' desks so they are seated in rows when class begins and then have students move into their small groups when you call for it. (Typically students are noisier when they're in groups, so using rows to get class started may help you begin in a calmer way.) In fact, you can make this change in the middle of a class period; don't feel obligated to wait until the start of a new grading period.

Sometimes, it isn't necessary to completely change the rules and procedures. Instead, it may be appropriate to apply consequences when students don't adhere to rules and procedures (Marzano, 2007, 2017). Classroom management is often the area of teaching that causes the most stress for beginning teachers. Knowing how and when to adequately respond to disruptions in class is an essential skill that you can deliberately practice early on in the school year.

These classroom management strategies might be helpful during this phase (Marzano, 2007, 2017).

- **Extended pause:** When you notice students not following a rule or procedure while you're engaging in direct instruction, simply pause for a moment. It draws attention to the break in the flow. This allows you to calmly and respectfully cue the misbehaving students that you notice what is happening and will not continue until they correct their behavior. Imagine that you're talking to your class and notice something happening. Rather than redirecting or moving toward the disruption, you simply freeze, look in the direction of the problem, wait until the student corrects him- or herself, and then—only then—you continue.

- **Nonverbal cues:** Alongside and beyond the extended pause, nonverbal cues help redirect students. Those cues include a look of disapproval, a finger to your lips, a head shake no, and a closer stance. Again, you're not reprimanding students or majorly disrupting the lesson flow. Instead, you're giving students an opportunity to correct their own behavior by nonverbally reminding them of a rule or procedure.

- ◆ **Verbal cues:** If nonverbal cues aren't working, try verbal cues—move closer to the student, say his or her name, quietly explain that a rule is not being followed, and then remind the student of the behavior you want to see. Consider doing this privately, when possible, to avoid embarrassing the student or hurting your relationship. Move to the student, get on his or her level, make eye contact, and quietly have a direct conversation about the problem and what you need to see instead.

If these strategies don't seem to work and the students who don't follow rules and procedures continually frustrate you, it might be wise to revisit your original rules and procedures and ask yourself the following questions.

- ◆ "Have I determined that students know the rules and procedures?"

- ◆ "Are just a few students struggling or is it the majority? If the majority of my students are struggling, what rule or procedure might I modify?"

- ◆ "Do student behaviors change depending on the time of day or the day of the week? Do I need different rules and procedures for the afternoon than those for the morning? Do I need to remind students of the rules and procedures on Fridays?"

- ◆ "Is there someone else in the building I can ask to help me with my rules and procedures?"

Displaying Objectivity and Control

While dealing with classroom management issues, it is important to display objectivity and control. Objectivity and control mean that you don't view students as friends or as enemies, but as *learners* (Marzano Resources, n.d.). While it is important to be friendly and inviting, it is also important to be in control of your classroom. We have discussed the importance of relationships and rules and procedures; together, these elements can help you achieve this balance. Objectivity and control come across as calmness and directness. When dealing with a student who isn't adhering to the rules, you might say, "I care about you as a student and want you to succeed. To succeed in this class, I need you to follow the rules."

Reflection and mindful self-care practices can help you develop this skill. (See this chapter's reflection section, on page 47.) Remaining calm is easier if you can implement these ideas.

- **Being assertive:** When thinking about interactions, aim for assertiveness rather than being passive or aggressive. An assertive statement sounds something like this: "Eric, I cannot teach when you are talking with Brian. Please give me your full attention." Conversely, a passive statement sounds like this: "How many times do I have to ask you to pay attention, boys? It's time you started acting like seventh graders." An aggressive statement sounds like this: "I've had it with you! You never stop talking and disrupting the entire class! Stop it!" Being assertive means that you are "able to assert your own needs without ignoring or violating the rights of your students" (Marzano Resources, n.d.). Assertiveness does not ignore or punish negative behavior but addresses it in a respectful way that lets students know a behavior is unacceptable. Calmly point out that behavior and state clearly what you need to see instead.

- **Maintaining a cool exterior:** Be aware of your facial expressions and voice. Try to keep your face calm, rather than scowling, and keep your voice even, rather than yelling. Speak respectfully, listen carefully, and avoid power struggles. If a student tries to pull you into a power struggle, disengage in that moment and set up a time to speak to that student later. When you meet, employ the actively listening and speaking steps outlined next. This is a simple strategy but isn't always easy to employ, particularly in the heat of the moment. Being able to take a deep breath and re-center yourself is the cornerstone of this teacher move. I explain it in this chapter's self-care practices.

♦ **Actively listening and speaking:** It is important to listen to your students neutrally. Try to remain neutral and nonjudgmental, which means "trying not to take sides or form opinions, especially early in the conversation" ("Active listening," n.d.).

Use the following four steps to practice active listening and speaking.

1. After hearing what a student says, paraphrase what you heard. Sample sentence starters for paraphrasing include, *Let me make sure that I understand what you're saying, Tell me if this is correct,* and *In other words.*

2. Ask if your understanding is correct. If your understanding is incorrect, ask the student to tell you again.

3. If you understand correctly, ask the student to continue.

4. Continue this cycle until the student is finished and calmer.

Don't jump to conclusions, make assumptions, internally form a response while the student's speaking, or interject. Don't provide your own interpretation of why a student is behaving this way.

Noticing When Students Are Not Engaged

When are your students engaged? When are they disengaged? How do you know? There is a distinct difference between compliance and engagement. Compliant students are quiet, sit still, and aren't causing distractions. Engaged students are thinking about the content and actively learning. You can check whether students are compliant or truly engaged by doing the following.

- Scan the room for body language clues. Are students sitting up straight or are they slouching?

- Listen to small-group conversations. Are students on task or are they talking about their weekend plans?

- Work with students one-to-one while they work independently. Ask them what they're thinking about, what questions they have, or what interests them about the content they're working on.

You might even consider asking students to monitor their own levels of engagement. You can do this in a few different ways. You can periodically have students respond to a statement like, "OK, class, I need you to check into your own engagement level right now. Please use your fingers to show me. Zero means not at all engaged and five means you're highly engaged." Or have them keep cards at their desks and show a red card when they need help or feel unengaged, a yellow card when they're moderately engaged, and a green card when they're highly engaged (Marzano, 2012). For older students, simply asking them to pause and reflect on their own engagement can be effective.

If you notice or students report a lack of engagement, use one of the strategies in chapter 4, on page 69, and chapter 5, on page 83. For now, during this phase, focus on building your awareness. That awareness helps us think beyond our own behaviors and pay attention to how students are responding to the lesson at hand. By learning to pay attention to that aspect, you will start considering whether your teaching strategies have the desired effect on your students.

Self-Care Practices

Hopefully, you've maintained the foundational self-care practices that you established during the anticipation phase. Keep them going through the survival phase, if you can. Now, more than ever, you need adequate sleep; healthy, high-energy foods; and physical activity that feels good to you. While it is tempting to let some of your good habits go so you can focus on classroom demands, I urge you to keep up those good habits. Your foundational habits are essential aspects of your teaching life. If you slip a bit, forgive yourself and attempt to get back on track as quickly as possible. Commit to taking one baby step toward a more balanced you. Now I'm going to introduce you to a few more practices that might be acutely helpful during this phase. Practicing mindfulness and focusing on relationships help keep the other important aspects of your life in sight. Remember that these are recommendations rather than requirements. As you read, consider and implement only what appeals to you.

Practicing Mindfulness

Mindfulness is a term that seems to be everywhere—and for good reason. The benefits of mindfulness, which people most often practice as meditation, include everything from slowing down automatic reactions to stressful situations (Tang et al., 2007) to maintaining positive social relationships (Carson, Carson, Gil, & Baucom, 2004). Additional research shows that mindfulness can help humans cope, reduce anxiety, and improve overall well-being. Mindfulness may also reduce emotional exhaustion and improve job satisfaction (Hülsheger, Alberts, Feinholdt, & Lang, 2013). Mindfulness practice also increases your ability to respond more effectively to complex or difficult situations and with more resilience (Lin, 2009). All of these benefits will help you as a new educator. According to Jon Kabat-Zinn (1994), who is a scientist and founding executive director of the Center for Mindfulness in Medicine, Health Care, and Society at the University of Massachusetts Medical School, "Mindfulness means paying attention in a particular way: on purpose, in the present moment, and nonjudgmentally" (p. 4). Stated differently, you can think of mindfulness as a particular way of paying attention. There are a variety of ways to engage in mindfulness. Setting an intention, meditating, mindful walking, and tactical breathing are all effective.

Setting an Intention

When you set an intention, you state what you want to get out of the day or how you want to behave or feel that day. This helps increase your mindfulness:

> When you set an intention, you are more
> likely to make choices that support it—in

what you do or what you think. You might
forget all about your intention today, but
some little part of your mind remembers it.
(Aguilar, 2014)

How cool is that? Your mind will remember your intention and
help you achieve it. I often set an intention like one of these in
the morning: *Today, I want to be fully present, Today I want to ask
questions, Today I want to connect deeply with others*, or even, *Today
I will be patient with Harry* (our sweet puppy who can drive me
bananas sometimes).

After you've set your intention, you might also identify what
it will look or sound like to hold, or recall, that intention. If my
intention is to be fully present today, I picture myself only checking my phone during breaks and lunch and after school, and holding eye contact with anyone I speak with. On days that I intend
to be more patient with my dog, Harry, I think about how I will
not yell and how I will be purposely grateful for all the uncondi-
tional love he brings to our lives. As you think about how to hold
your intention, envision how you want to feel and this particular
intention's best possible outcome.

You might record your intention at the top of your agenda each
day or on a sticky note (that's what I do) and keep it in your pocket
or near where you teach. The following intentions can get you
started in this practice. Use the spaces on page 44 to record your
own ideas.

- ◆ I want to be fully present so that I feel connected
  with my students and colleagues.

- ◆ I want to take risks so that I can increase my use
  of instructional expertise.

- ◆ I want to listen more than I speak so that I am
  open to learning from others.

- ◆ I want to connect with others so that I feel part of
  a community.

- ◆ I want to stay calm when interacting with
  certain colleagues or students so that the day can
  be peaceful.

- I want to ask hard questions so that I can be open to new ideas and share my own thinking.

- I want to be mindful of my breathing so that I can be more relaxed throughout the day.

- _____

_____

- _____

_____

Meditating

Hear me out on this one. I know that it may feel intimidating to try meditation. Or perhaps you've tried it but couldn't quiet your racing thoughts and so you quit. That's normal! And it's worth trying meditation again. It took me years, literally, of starting and stopping meditation before it finally stuck. Establishing a regular meditation practice can change your outlook on you, your life, and the world. In fact, meditation only requires that you take a seat and pay attention to your breath. That's truly it. When your mind wanders (or your racing thoughts kick in), simply return to your breath. Again and again. And then again. Start with one or two minutes and see if you can build up to ten minutes every single day. I think it's helpful to utilize guided meditations (where someone instructs you through the meditation, reminding you of your posture, breath, and focus) and highly recommend checking out the following applications: Calm, Get Grounded, and Headspace. All of these applications provide guided meditations of various lengths. They also have simple timers if you prefer to meditate on your own, without a voice guiding you. Visit **go.SolutionTree .com/instruction** for live links to these and some of my other favorite applications.

- Calm at www.calm.com
- Get Grounded on Apple at www.apple.co/2lS1IYA
- Headspace at www.headspace.com/headspace -meditation-app

Try getting up just five minutes earlier than usual all week. Do a quick meditation before you start your school day, and see if you notice in yourself different reactions to challenging situations and people. I'm willing to bet that you do. I meditate every morning, even if it's only for two minutes, and truly notice a difference. I am able to approach the day with a greater sense of calm than when I'm running around like a crazy person all morning long.

Mindful Walking

During your lunch break or planning period, challenge yourself to take a mindful walk—either around your building or outside if you can. Mindful walking is similar to a seated meditation and has many of the same benefits but instead of sitting still, you're moving. By taking a mindful walk, you are helping to strengthen your concentration, awareness, and connection to the present moment (Brady, n.d.), not to mention getting a little bit of exercise.

To practice this, simply pay attention to each step that you take. Maybe count your steps, see how slowly you can walk, or take longer breaths and longer strides. Halt the mental to-do list and instead, focus on your feet hitting the ground, the surrounding sounds, and your breath.

Tactical Breathing

Learning to control your breathing is an essential tool for staying calm, even during times of high stress in your classroom. Military members use tactical breathing to calm and center themselves in crisis situations (U.S. Navy, n.d.). I engage in tactical breathing multiple times a day, every day—particularly when I have a lot going on or feel especially stressed. You can try it yourself throughout the day. It is essential to displaying objectivity and control.

To try tactical breathing yourself, relax yourself by taking three to five breaths as I describe in the following four steps. Visualize each number as you count.

1.   Breathe in while silently counting, "One, two, three, four."

2.   Pause and hold your breath while silently counting, "One, two, three, four."

3. Exhale slowly while silently counting, "One, two, three, four."

4. Repeat this pattern.

Additionally, you may want to place your hands on your belly button and close your eyes while you breathe. When you inhale, your stomach should expand and when you exhale, your stomach should relax. When you don't have time to take even three deep breaths, simply pausing long enough to take one full breath can be impactful. Consider when it might be helpful to pause and engage in tactical breathing.

- When you transition from the parking lot to the school in the morning
- When you transition from your car to your house at the end of the day
- Before a particularly challenging class period
- Before a parent meeting
- Before a department meeting

By pausing to take a mindful breath, you can slow yourself down and approach a situation from a place of greater calm.

Focusing on Relationships

While you are wading through the survival phase, it is so incredibly important not to isolate yourself. As human beings, we are wired for connection (Cook, 2013). In fact, "people who are socially isolated are more likely to die prematurely" (Mohan, 2013). It can be easy to shut yourself off from your friends and family members because of time demands and constantly being surrounded by other people—colleagues, students, and parents.

Allow yourself to connect with someone outside of your professional world. Schedule time for personal relationships on the weekend or, if possible, during the workweek. Double up on your self-care and make a regular exercise date with a good friend, since exercise is an essential anticipation phase strategy. Seek out friends and family who are positive and supportive. When you are with those people, utilize your active listening to be fully present and engaged.

Reflections

Set aside time each day to reflect. The following prompts, related to classroom strategies and self-care practices for this phase in your first year, encourage this reflection. You don't need to respond to all of these in one sitting. Instead, dig into one or two at a time. Use the space at the end of this chapter to write about any other concerns or celebrations that you notice during the survival phase.

Classroom Strategy Prompts

Consider the following prompts in light of the survival phase.

- If I had to rate myself on a scale of one to ten— with one being terrible and ten being perfect— what number would I give myself for classroom management? Is it smooth sailing or am I desperate for additional support? Who might be able to help me? Have I received feedback from my administrator, coach, or mentor about my classroom management? Does their feedback mirror how I perceive my classroom? What would need to happen for me to move to the next level—not all the way to a ten, but improve just one number?

- Do I feel adequately in control of my classroom? Have I found that sweet spot between friend and authoritarian? Do I feel comfortable seeking feedback from my students? Can I ask them how they view me as a teacher?

- What is the difference between compliance and engagement? How do I know if my students are really engaged or if they're simply complying? Without embarrassing them, how can I ask students whether they're engaged?

- Is there a certain day or moment in which I truly feel energized in the classroom? What contributed to that feeling? How can I replicate that?

Self-Care Practice Prompts

Consider the following prompts in light of the survival phase.

- Am I comfortable setting an intention and engaging in meditation, including a mindful walk? If I haven't tried a mindfulness practice, what holds me back? (If you haven't attempted one, challenge yourself to one this week and be sure to record here how you felt before and after.)

- Does tactical breathing make sense to me? Do I notice my breath throughout the day? Do I typically notice my breath in my chest more than my stomach? During what times of day would mindful breathing be most beneficial? How will I remind myself to engage in mindful breathing?

- Who are the five most important people in my life? How much time do I spend communicating with them? Has the amount of time I spend with these important people drastically changed since I started teaching? Is there one person in particular who I can make time for?

— NOTES —

CHAPTER 3

The Disillusionment Phase

Now I need to acknowledge something dreadful so we can work through it: the disillusionment phase is a reality for nearly every beginning teacher that I know. It typically occurs around November. I wish that weren't the case, but it is. You start to lose your footing during the survival phase and fall face down during disillusionment. And it hurts. You may feel like you've hit the wall and struggle to make it day by day—or even hour by hour. You might begin to question your commitment, capabilities, and perhaps even your self-worth during this phase. It is not uncommon to fall ill (again) during this time. There's a chance your self-care practices have fallen by the wayside because you are completely overwhelmed with school right now. It's going to take all of your resolve, a lot of support, and the right combination of grit and perseverance to move out of this phase. But you can do it. I *know* you can do it.

You are not alone. Look around. I'm willing to bet other—even veteran—teachers are also experiencing the impact. I remember feeling very alone during this time. I felt as though everyone around me was doing just fine and that my exasperation meant something was wrong with me. But here's the truth: this job is extremely tough. Everything is new. You don't have a lot of automaticity, and having to deliberately practice every detail of every day is exhausting. You're not doing anything wrong; there is no defect in you. This is simply part of the process. Here's what helps: focusing on the important things, including the relationships you have with your students, your support system, and yourself. Remind yourself again (and again) that busy doesn't mean better. Drowning in work, staying at school until late into the evening, and completely losing yourself to your job isn't helping anyone, including your students. Resist the one-upmanship that can exist among colleagues. If someone shares how many hours he is working and the next person exclaims that she is working even *more* hours, simply remove yourself from the conversation.

In chapter 2, on page 33, I shared my disillusionment phase story in hopes of providing a heads-up about where you probably are right now. Here, I'm going to share my reflection phase story to remind you that it really does get better. You will get through this. This phase will not last forever. With kindness, patience, and perseverance, things will change. Do not give up. We need you; your students need you.

What a Difference a Year Makes

During the third quarter of the first year I taught, someone handed me a vocabulary book and told me to use it in the classroom. I panicked. There were twenty words in each unit. There were twenty units in the book. There were tests after every unit, and a unit review after every third unit, followed by a larger review of the preceding six units. *I* didn't even know some of the words! Until that point, I gave vocabulary lessons in my middle school classroom in an authentic setting, while we were working on something else. I'd introduce about five new words a week, have students create flash cards with pictures and funny sentences to help them remember the word, and give a short quiz every once in a while to check retention. Admittedly, vocabulary on its own was not my major focus. In our third quarter, I handed out the little orange books, asked students to put their names in permanent marker everywhere they could, and explained our new vocabulary program. As Johnny took out his marker and began to write his name on every single page of the book, the other students groaned openly. I hid my own groans.

We did a unit a week. Yup—twenty new words a week. Definitions, parts of speech, synonyms, antonyms, and pronunciations. I mostly assigned it as homework because we simply did not have time to do the work in class. I'm certain some copied one another's work; most students didn't finish the work. I handed out the tests on Friday and wasn't surprised when the students did poorly. So, I put on my stern teacher face and told the students that they were going to need to work harder. "Study five words a night," I stressed. "Make flash cards!" I yelled. "This is a big part of your grade," I threatened. Week two was no better. In fact, I believe it was worse.

What was my alternative? I had to use the book, and I only had forty-five minutes a day to cover reading, writing, and (now) a vocabulary unit. I kept pushing. I required flash cards for students who failed tests, I offered extra help before and after school (only two students showed up), and I called home to beg for support. Week three was worse. The review test was downright heartbreaking.

But I got through the entire book, darn it. I marched up to my department head, showed her the completed book with pride, and when she asked me how it went, I burst into tears. My students had not retained one single word from the book. The little orange cover became a negative trigger. Parents could not believe the amount of work that I was requiring at home when until that point I had been so reasonable. I was mad—mad that I had to use this book and even angrier that I had failed so miserably at the task.

My department head patted me on the back, just as she had so many times that year, and applauded my efforts. Then she asked me what I would do differently next year. I explained that for starters, I'd want the book at the beginning of the year. Next, I'd teach only ten words per week. I'd cut the accent mark portion of the test because I couldn't understand why students needed to know which syllable was stressed on top of knowing the spelling, definition, and part of speech. I told her that I thought the words were valuable, but the setup was a disaster.

I waited for her to tell me that she was sorry but I was just going to have to deal with it. Guess what? She didn't say that.

She recalled her own experience, when she did everything that was given to her, no questions asked. She explained that she had used the very same book but completed only the first ten units. Like me, she felt that the accent mark part was ridiculous, so she threw it out. Threw it out? You can just throw it out? I was astonished. She said that if twenty words were too many, I could teach ten like she had. Teach the other ten the following week. When she asked if it was more important to get through the entire book or for students to learn new vocabulary, I stated the obvious answer—but, someone told me I had to get through the entire book. "Oh, Tina, bless your heart. You'll learn." And then she sailed off like the Wizard of Oz, and I was left speechless, holding the little orange book that had nearly crushed me.

I began to understand. After recently graduating from university, where assignments weren't ever optional, I was now in a profession where I was handed a few resources and told simply to use them. I wanted to be the best. In my mind, being the best meant completing required tasks, even though I knew my students weren't learning and it conflicted with what I wanted to do in class. It hadn't dawned on me that I could change things. This is going to happen to you, too. You'll have been teaching for a decade when you look back and chuckle at the things you used to do. Someday the confidence fairy bestows a valuable lesson at the heart of teaching: always ask yourself, "What is the best way to allow students to learn to the best of their abilities?"

The following year, we still did not get our vocabulary books until the third quarter. This time, though, I knew they were coming. From the year's start, I set up our vocabulary unit to mirror the book. I also focused on only half the words per week, taking twice the time to get through the book. I even incorporated a little bit of fun into these dry words. For example, if I heard the students using the words correctly (without the aid of their books) outside class, I'd award them an extra point. Suddenly, the hallway was filled with conversations like, "Is Mrs. Langer's class the one that is *adjacent* to the cafeteria?" or "I wish they'd *decrease* the amount of homework we have on the weekend." I also tried to immerse students in their new words, cutting out magazine articles that used their words, asking them to do the same, and handing out each week's list to the elective teachers and asking them to use the words whenever possible. We'd spend ten minutes on Fridays playing a review game that students created. I'd made it a contest to see who could create the best review game. And when the tests came around, my students did well.

At the end of my second year, I handed the book to my department head and announced with a show-off smile that I had completed only half the book. She gave me a high five and told me I was becoming an official teacher. I beamed.

Prompts

As you learn about strategies and practices in this chapter, consider the following questions.

What might I be able to relax on to ensure depth of learning and retention rather than rote memorization?

How do I prioritize students' learning goals?

How might I ease up on myself, especially during the disillusionment phase?

Classroom Strategies

You are in the most difficult phase of the entire school year and so we are going to proceed with caution here. When I work with beginning teacher mentors, I gently remind them not to bombard new teachers with complicated data during this phase. Instead, you need kindness, compassion, and gentle support.

I've selected the classroom strategies that I believe will help you the most right now: developing relationships with all students, celebrating students' successes, and focusing on positive student behaviors. These strategies are about the heart of your work and will gently remind you of the important parts: your students, precious human beings who need love above all else (no matter how old they are) and their growth. I also chose these strategies because they help your brain focus on what's going *right* rather than solely on what isn't. Deliberately practice these strategies, but also remember one of the simplest, most powerful ones we've discussed: greet students at the door each day. You will feel more centered and connected if you say each student's name and greet him or her with a simple "Hello" and a handshake. This greeting also helps further develop or maintain a positive relationship with each student, which is essential.

Developing Relationships With All Students

During the disillusionment phase in particular, I highly, highly recommend that your main focus be on building relationships with students (and I have selected strategies that emphasize this). These relationships can help sustain you during even the most difficult times. I suspect that you got into education because you love children. Now is the time to remember that, above all else. If students don't feel supported by you, they're not going to learn the content as easily. Relationships *absolutely* impact student engagement (Pianta, Hamre, & Stuhlman, 2003; Roorda, Koomen, Spilt, & Oort, 2011).

While you're at home, on a walk, or driving to or from school, think about each of your students. Do you know something academic and nonacademic about each of them? If there are students you aren't as connected with, consider setting up one-to-one time with each of them. This could happen before or after school, or during lunch or individual classwork time. During this conference, you might ask the student questions or use discussion prompts that will help you get to know him or her more deeply (Marzano Resources, n.d.).

- How is class going? What is working well and what isn't?

- Tell me about your family.

- What do you like? Do you like sports, music, movies, books, or hobbies?

- Tell me about your friends.

- What are the moments of your life that you are proudest of, both in and outside of school?

- What are your dreams and goals?

- What are your weekend plans?
- What are you excited about?

Intentionally relating to all of your students may make classroom management easier. Students are much more willing to follow the rules and procedures if they have a sense of trust and respect for the teacher (Sparks, 2016). Robert J. Marzano (2017) asserts "using verbal and nonverbal behaviors that indicate affection for students" builds trust and respect, because the things we say (verbally) and the behaviors we engage in (nonverbally) are both important aspects of any relationship (p. 89). More specifically, you know that verbal behaviors like greeting students at the door and scheduling time to get to know them better work. Spur-of-the-moment interactions also work. Ask students in the hallway about their days. Students typically enjoy sharing details about themselves.

Often your quietest students want most to be heard. Don't stop talking to them if they appear shy or reticent. These students may have stopped sharing because, somewhere along the way, no one was really listening. If you keep trying, they just may open up to you. On the other hand, you might discover that students are facing challenges that you feel unprepared or unqualified to fix. Remember that you don't have to solve their problems. Contact your school's counselors or social workers if you discover something alarming when you're working with a student. Your listening is a gift and lets them know that their voices matter.

Nonverbal behaviors beyond smiling, nodding, high-fiving, fist-bumping, or patting a student on the back also include attending after-school events like games or performances. Students love to see you in the crowd cheering them on. I also understand that this is an additional time commitment. You don't have to stay for the entire time. Simply making an appearance is enough to demonstrate that you care about your students as people. Take photos at the events so you can share them with students, mention specific aspects of their performances the next day, or write simple notes of acknowledgment to them as a way of connecting even further. This is an especially important thing to consider for students who do not have support at home or whose situations make it difficult for parents or guardians to attend these events.

Do you remember the first time you saw your teacher outside of the school? I do. I remember being so confused as to how this person could be anywhere outside of our classroom, and I was shocked at the realization that this person also shopped for groceries and ate dinner at restaurants! I felt so honored for this person—this hero of mine—to recognize me and to talk to me in aisle three of the Hy-Vee grocery store. If you see students outside of school, unexpectedly—and you will—at the grocery store, movies, or a restaurant, it is important to say hello. Use the student's name when greeting him or her. This simple act shows that you like your students and enjoy seeing them.

Humor is another one of my favorite relationship development strategies. Students often report their favorite teacher is the one who makes them laugh while they learn. Think about it: when you attend a class or a professional development session, don't you feel better about the time and the instructor if you're laughing? Being able to laugh at yourself, inserting jokes into your classes, sharing funny pictures or headlines, and genuinely giggling at the funny stories your students tell you make both you and your students feel good! Use that to your advantage, especially during the disillusionment phase. Be careful to avoid sarcasm; it can be considered cruel and can spiral out of control; students typically don't catch on (Gatens, 2014).

Celebrating Students' Successes

During this phase, it can be easy to feel like your students aren't making the progress that you want them to make. Perhaps you've had to reteach a lesson or a concept many times and still they aren't grasping it. Maybe your colleagues are further along in their instructional units. It's OK. Your students will get there. The truth of the matter is, your students *are* making progress; it just might feel like really *slow* progress. To boost your students' confidence—as well as your own—celebrate their successes, even small ones. You can certainly celebrate at the end of a unit, but I also recommend focusing on growth. How much progress have they made from the beginning to the end of a unit? For now, disregard whether they're proficient yet. Focus on growth instead.

One way to track growth and celebrate is by using proficiency scales for each unit. Perhaps your school uses them already. If not, start with a generic, student-friendly assessment scale that you can use with any instructional unit. After students know what the learning goals are, you can use a scale like the one in figure 3.1.

Score 4	I know it and can teach a friend about it.
Score 3	I know it just the way my teacher taught it.
Score 2	I know some of the simpler stuff but can't do the hard parts.
Score 1	With some help, I can do it.
Score 0	Even with help, I can't do it.

Figure 3.1: Formative assessment scale.

*Visit **go.SolutionTree.com/instruction** for a free reproducible version of this figure.*

To utilize this scale, begin by sharing the specific learning goals at the beginning of a new unit. Ask students to record their scores at that point. Reassure them that it's perfectly fine to have a low score and that the goal is to learn together and move up the scale. Then, periodically throughout the unit, you can ask students to revisit their original scores and mark their new scores as their learning progresses. You can do this formally, in students' own academic notebooks, or informally, by having them show you their scores with their fingers or on a note at the end of the day. Then, throughout or at the unit's end, you can celebrate students whose scores increased. Highlight the hard work it took them to improve. You can do this with individual students or with the class as a whole.

Celebrate students in a variety of ways, including public or one-to-one acknowledgment, phone calls, or letters home. You can look your student in the eye, shake his or her hand, and say how proud you are and why. It's important to know what type of recognition each student will most likely appreciate. For example, to celebrate me, you can throw a big party and put my name on a giant billboard; I'll love it! To celebrate my husband, on the other hand, it's best to keep it low key and personal. You have students like us and those in between. If you're not sure of the best way to acknowledge a student, simply ask. Start with a one-to-one conversation during which you praise his or her growth, discuss what the student did to achieve that growth, and then suggest that you'd like to celebrate the student another way. Ask if any of the following options sound good to him or her: a phone call home, recognition in front of the class, or something else.

Focusing on Positive Student Behaviors

It's easy to notice when students *aren't* doing what they're supposed to be doing—but it's equally, if not more, important to recognize when they *are*. Pointing out these positives sets a warm tone and reinforces the desired behaviors in a positive way. It feels good to praise students and, per seminal psychologist and behaviorist B. F. Skinner (1948), praise typically leads to even better behavior.

You can acknowledge adherence to rules and procedures many ways, but you might begin with the following ideas. Use the spaces on page 61 to record your own ideas.

- ◆ Show appreciation for individual students or the entire class by using phrases such as, "Thank you," "Good job," and "I appreciate . . ." followed by a brief but specific description of the desired behavior. This might sound like, "Thank you for being such attentive listeners today," or "I appreciate the way you're sticking with this project," or "I'm so proud of how well you guys are working in groups right now" (Marzano, 2017).

- ◆ Smiles, nods, and other nonverbal cues can go a long way toward helping you focus on positive behaviors and establishing a warm classroom atmosphere with solid relationships at the core (Marzano, 2017).

- ◆ Write down what you appreciate about students. Students can keep these notes or show their parents or guardians. When I utilized this strategy, I was amazed to see those well-worn notes still in their folders at the end of the year.

List your ideas here.

◆   _____

     _____

◆   _____

     _____

Self-Care Practices

As you are keenly aware by now, the disillusionment phase is tough. Keep up with the self-care routine that you've established. If you're getting less sleep, aren't exercising, or aren't eating well, reread chapter 1 (page 13) and remind yourself how good you feel when you're doing these things.

In addition to those core self-care practices—which might include simply walking around the block in the evening or adding a vegetable to your plate at dinner—consider a few more practices that might be particularly helpful when you're struggling. My suggestions include practicing gratitude, practicing kindness, and appreciating humor. Bring as much of these to your life outside the classroom as you can. Read through the following strategies and consider which appeal the most to you.

Practicing Gratitude

When we intentionally recognize what's going well in our lives, it takes us out of our misery for a few moments and reminds us of the bigger picture. In my own journal, I record what I'm grateful for each week, and I do so mentally at the end of a particularly challenging day. I always feel better when I remember how grateful I am for the way my puppy snuggles with me when he's tired or how thankful I am that my husband cleaned the house for us or how beautiful the mountains look when I take my early morning walks. It will likely work for you, too, because "people who regularly practice gratitude by taking time to notice and reflect upon the things they're thankful for experience more positive emotions, feel more alive, sleep better, express more compassion and kindness, and even have stronger immune systems" (Carpenter, n.d.).

At the beginning of the day during trainings, I often ask participating educators to share something they're grateful for. It sets a positive tone and helps shift the grumpy mood that typically comes with mandatory training.

As with any new practice, it takes time to make the habit stick. To start your own gratitude practice, record here three things that you're grateful for today.

- ◆ _____

- ◆ _____

- ◆ _____

Try the following suggestions as you get started (Russell, n.d.).

- ◆ **Commit:** When you're in the throes of the disillusionment phase, this might feel like just another thing you have to do. Ignore this thought. This takes a few minutes at most. By recognizing all the things you're grateful for, you'll start to feel different. And yes, you can even be grateful for strong coffee and good TV shows.

- ◆ **Write it down:** By recording your gratitude statements in writing, rather than mentally only, you have a record of your key learnings and growth. Plus, you have something to look back on when things invariably get tough again.

- ◆ **Choose a set time:** To help make this a habit, set aside a certain time of day or week to record your gratitude thoughts. You can combine this practice with setting intentions and write at the beginning of the day, write at night so you can fall asleep feeling positive, or write on a Friday or Sunday to reflect on your week as a whole—reflecting on both your personal and professional lives.

- ◆ **Practice present-moment gratitude:** Recognize feelings of gratitude in the moment as a way to help maintain calm and peace throughout the day. Acknowledge these moments in real time. When a student thanks you for something, or is kind to another student, pausing for a moment to say a silent thanks can make you feel better instantly.

◆ **Share the gratitude:** Consider sharing your list with a friend, colleague, or mentor, if it feels comfortable. Some teams and entire school staffs start meetings with each person sharing what he or she is grateful for in that moment.

◆ **Keep going:** Don't stop once you see results. Even when you move out of the disillusionment phase, it is important to continue this practice. Keep the momentum.

◆ **Allow yourself to be human:** Some days will be more difficult than others and that's OK. You may just need to write *I am grateful I am writing my gratitude list* three times. Tomorrow is a new day.

Beyond journaling, you might consider other ways to demonstrate gratitude in your daily life.

◆ **Use sticky notes to spread messages:** Write what you're grateful for and post the notes throughout your classroom, school, and home.

◆ **Write and deliver thank-you notes:** Give them to particularly helpful colleagues, friends, or family members. You can do this via email or text message, too. I'm just particularly fond of a good old-fashioned handwritten note.

◆ **Go on a gratitude walk:** Record or draw what you are thankful for as you're out exploring. Consider combining this with a mindfulness walk, which I describe in chapter 2, on page 33.

◆ **Share your gratitude through social media:** Snap a photo of something you're thankful for and share that image with one word: *gratitude*. Share your gratitude with your students and ask them to do the same.

- **Keep a gratitude jar:** Record one thing you are grateful for each day on a piece of paper and place it in the jar. At the end of the school or calendar year, read each note and reminisce. Students love this activity and it's perfectly fine to not have started at the very beginning of the school year; simply start when you can.

- **Thank yourself:** Write yourself a letter where you celebrate all that you've accomplished so far. After all, you're still here. Think of what you'd say to friends to help them feel better and use those same words to celebrate yourself.

Are you grateful for your warm bed? Your understanding family or friends? Your mentor? The way your third period class appreciates your jokes? Write it down.

Practicing Kindness

When you are feeling particularly low, as one often does during the disillusionment phase, commit to engaging in one small act of kindness each day or each week. This could be something you do for a student, a parent, a colleague, or yourself and could be as simple as giving someone a genuine compliment or contacting the family of one of your students to share a success story on behalf of the student. You could also treat yourself to a special coffee or other treat for no particular reason other than that you deserve it! At the Random Acts of Kindness website (www.randomactsofkindness.org/printables), there are free downloadable calendars with a simple idea every day that can be an excellent starting place for you. Additionally, this website contains lesson plans if you'd like to extend this self-care practice into your classroom.

Consider the following additional ways that you can incorporate acts of kindness into your daily life.

- Post a sticky note on someone's desk, door, or locker with a positive message.
- Pay for someone else's coffee.

- Buy someone else—or yourself—a small bouquet of flowers for no particular reason.

- Engage in mindful listening when talking with someone else today. (Give him or her your full attention rather than attempting to do something else while engaged in the conversation.)

- Pass along a great book that you've read to someone else who might also enjoy it.

- Compliment a friend or colleague.

- Put a surprise note in your partner or child's lunch today.

- Support local businesses.

Appreciating Humor

Humor was one of the ways I suggested developing positive relationships with your students. It's also something that I recommend you consider outside of the classroom. Humor and laughter are essential in helping us through difficult times. Think about times in your life when you were in a difficult situation and suddenly something made you laugh and you felt an incredible sense of relief. That's the power of laughter. Brené Brown (n.d.) reminds us that "laughter is a spiritual form of communing. Without words we say to one another, 'I'm with you. I get it.'" Make it a priority to laugh every single day. Yes, you read that correctly: every single day. Whether it's appreciating the humor of your students, being able to laugh at yourself, or watching a funny video clip, TV show, or movie, remember that humor can positively impact your life, correlates with increased productivity, reduces stress, and promotes creative thinking (Jonas, 2010).

Here are some ways you might incorporate humor into your life.

- Bookmark websites that make you laugh and take two minutes in the morning to review them. Some of my favorites follow.

  ◇ The Chive (www.thechive.com) includes funny pictures, videos, memes, and photographs.

⬦ Funny or Die (www.funnyordie.com) features hilarious sketches from comedians and celebrities.

⬦ The Oatmeal (www.theoatmeal.com) has endearing and funny comics by Matthew Inman.

⬦ The Onion (www.theonion.com) features satirical news stories.

♦ Watch a sitcom rather than the news at night. Psychologist Graham Davey warns, "Negative news can significantly change an individual's mood—especially if there is a tendency in the news broadcasts to emphasize suffering and also the emotional components of the story" (as cited in Gregoire, 2015).

♦ Keep a file for clippings, stories, pictures, memes, and jokes that make you smile. Add to this file as often as you can and dig into it when you need a good chuckle.

♦ Buy humorous or joke books to read on a regular basis.

♦ Don't be afraid to laugh at yourself.

♦ Watch a funny movie.

♦ Go to a comedy club or an improvisational show.

♦ Surround yourself with people who make you smile, laugh, and feel good.

Reflections

Set aside time each day to reflect. The following prompts, related to classroom strategies and self-care practices for this phase in your first year, encourage this reflection. You don't need to respond to all of these in one sitting. Instead, dig into one or two at a time. Use the space at the end of this chapter to write about any other concerns or celebrations that you notice during the disillusionment phase.

Classroom Strategy Prompts

Consider the following prompts in light of the disillusionment phase.

- When I reflect on my students as human beings, rather than as learners, what do I appreciate most about each one? What positive stories do I share about them with my family and friends?

- How often do I celebrate my students' successes? Which students might not be proficient with a learning target but have made significant gains? Have I recognized them? Have I told my students that I am proud of them? Have I talked with them about what they've done to contribute to my own growth?

- How many times have I recognized positive student behavior? How does that compare to how many times I've responded to negative student behavior? Can I try increasing the positives this week? Is there a particularly challenging student who I can commit to catching doing something right?

- Have I celebrated my own growth? How? If I haven't, what prevented me from doing so?

Self-Care Practice Prompts

Consider the following prompts in light of the disillusionment phase.

- How is my gratitude practice going? (Pause right now and record three things that you're grateful for in this very moment. Make a note on your calendar to do this again in a week.)

- When did someone show me kindness this week? Have I thanked that person? When did I show someone else kindness? How did it make me feel? How can I share kindness tomorrow?

- When was the last time I laughed? How did it feel? What made me laugh, and what do I find funny?

– NOTES –

CHAPTER 4

The Rejuvenation Phase

Pause for a moment to celebrate the fact that you're out of the disillusionment phase! Woo-hoo! You survived! You're on the upswing now! Doesn't it feel good? Bask in the glory. Sometimes you thought you wouldn't make it, but you did. You're here. Welcome to the rejuvenation phase. Typically, this phase shows up after winter break, when you've had more time outside of school to rest and spend with friends and family. Now you're back at school, feeling refreshed and more stable in your quest to make it through your first year. You might have an entirely new outlook on teaching and your own accomplishments. This phase is full of hope and will carry you through to the upcoming reflection phase.

The essay that I share for this phase is a fun one because in it I talk about play. I explain *brain breaks*, which occur when teachers shift the current activity to something that works a different part of the brain. They should last just a few minutes and require little or no equipment so that they're energizing but not chaotic.

Playing Can Be Productive

Get on your feet. Turn on some music. Dance. Play! If you play with your students, and I mean really play, you're bound to end the day with a smile, and your students will walk out of your room having learned something. It doesn't matter if you teach kindergarteners or seniors; everyone likes to play. And if you're all having fun, the learning will come naturally.

You might feel a little foolish at first—especially if you're dealing with "I'm way too cool for this" secondary students—but once you get over the first minute, your students will join you. Trust me on this one. Have students learn new facts by making up a song. Let them join small groups to make up the song, or ask them to create it as a whole class. Stand in a large circle and pass facts around as quickly as possible. Act out anything you possibly can. Have the students teach one another. Throw a dance party the last two minutes of class. Any time that you can be up, moving around, and active, you're bound to get positive results. I still can remember the song we sang in elementary school to learn the major math functions.

I've had my students act out social studies facts, writing and performing the scripts; they remember the events much more clearly than if they had simply read a textbook (Sousa 2017). I've had students perform fashion shows where they describe their (imagined or real) British fashion, who would have worn this outfit, and why. The students love it—and I do, too! I've set up our own private talk show in the style of Ellen DeGeneres in which various book characters are the guests (and of course we start with a dance segment, just like Ellen would want us to). Borrow ideas from game shows. Students love competing and acting the parts of host and contestants. Listen carefully in the hallways later in the day, and you'll hear your students singing their new song about hydrogen and oxygen, or practicing their runway walk in their extravagant British gowns.

As students, we've spent time (lots of time) trapped at our desks with our stone-faced teachers behind the podium spewing meaningless facts at us directly from the textbook. Ugh. We don't remember those facts, and we didn't enjoy our time in that classroom. Students need to get up and move and actively engage their brains—and guess what—so do we. If you're teaching in a setting where you'll perform the same lesson for four periods in a row, you need to energize yourself and your lesson to keep it fresh. Incorporating play into your lessons doesn't mean any more work—it means creativity. If you can't quite figure out how to make a lesson more creative, ask your students. They'll be full of brilliant ideas. Give them their learning objectives and empower them to come up with a creative way to learn them.

There will be standardized tests and serious days, of course, but whenever you have the opportunity to make things fun and exciting, do it. This works especially well at the end of a grading period or before a vacation because everyone will be antsy with the anticipation of some time away from school. This does not mean that you have to throw out the learning and pop in the latest Disney movie during class. Watching a movie in class can be worse than poking out your own eyeballs, trust me. Students don't want to sit and stare at the television when they're antsy, especially secondary students at a G-rated movie. Use their built-up energy to make up a fun lesson. Review the lessons of the quarter with a game show. All you need to do is provide a couple of snack-size candy bars as prizes, and every student in the room will be attentive and ready to play.

So try chanting or dancing or singing out your day's objective. Being able to do this is one serious advantage we have in this profession—use it!

Prompts

As you learn about strategies and practices in this chapter, consider the following questions.

When do students get to play in my classroom? Is it enough?

How can I get students moving and still thinking about content?

Can I incorporate more brain breaks?

Classroom Strategies

Moving out of disillusionment and into the rejuvenation phase feels great. Now that you're more settled and balanced, I present to you the following classroom strategies to focus on: demonstrating intensity and enthusiasm, utilizing physical movement, presenting unusual or intriguing information, and maintaining a lively pace as these strategies are essential for both learning content and engaging students.

Demonstrating Intensity and Enthusiasm

Demonstrating intensity and enthusiasm increases students' engagement levels (Marzano & Pickering, 2011). This incredible strategy is one of my favorites because it doesn't take extra time or resources. Instead, it is all about your demeanor. I recommend that you be enthusiastic all of the time and intense some of the time. Mirror neurons in our brain allow us to pick up on other people's emotions and this is especially true in the classroom (Winerman, 2005). The more excited you are, the more excited your students will be. If you want engaged, positive students, you must model those characteristics.

To clarify, I describe *enthusiasm* as your excitement and passion for the content you're teaching as well as for your students. You probably have memories of a teacher who legitimately loved his or her job and, as a result, helped you feel more connected to that teacher, class, and content. Conversely, you probably also have memories of teachers who did not appear to like their jobs, the content, or even the students. Remember these feelings? Being enthusiastic means your students feel that you love your job, you love them, and there's nowhere else in the world you'd rather be. This enthusiasm will go a long way in engaging students and helping them to learn the content.

Intensity, on the other hand, is a strategy you can use periodically to get students' attention. Intensity can involve verbal signals like the volume and tone of your voice and how you build anticipation and excitement for a topic by gesturing, smiling, and moving around the room while teaching (Marzano, 2012). When you say something like, "Today we are going to learn about character development in our writing. Now pay close attention and make sure that you understand exactly what I'm saying," you're being intense.

When you say to your students something like, "*You guys.* We're about to read this amazing book that I just *know* you're going to love, and I cannot wait to share it with you!" you are demonstrating both enthusiasm and intensity. Compare that statement to, "We're going to start this new book because it's the next thing on our curriculum map."

Big difference, right? Be the teacher who your students crave to be around.

Utilizing Physical Movement

The part of the brain that processes movement is the same part of the brain that processes learning (Jensen, 2005). This means that not only does physical movement help students stay alert and attentive, it also helps them learn (Donnelly & Lambourne, 2011). Think about how powerful that research is. The sad part is, we didn't always know this. If we did, our schools would most likely look significantly different than many of them do today.

Often, schools pull the students who need the most learning out of recess or physical education and give them a block schedule. We do this for all the right reasons (they need more time with reading, for example) but then they don't move their bodies for the block's entire ninety minutes. But now more teachers and administrators are aware of the research and the importance of incorporating physical movement (a type of brain break) into our classrooms on a daily basis—not simply during recess or physical education. Now that you have established clear classroom rules and procedures, incorporating movement into your class is simple. There are a variety of ways to get students up and moving (Marzano, 2012).

- **Stand and stretch:** Have students stand up next to their desks and stretch a bit to help to get more blood and oxygen to flow to the brain. Because this takes less than a minute, you can do this multiple times per class period. Use Go Noodle (www.gonoodle.com), a free website that provides fun guided-movement and mindfulness breaks for the classroom.

- **Get physical:** Take a break about every ten minutes with elementary students and about every twenty minutes with secondary students. Ask students to try these quickies.

    ◇ Do ten jumping jacks.

    ◇ Hold a plank pose for thirty seconds.

    ◇ Balance on one foot for thirty seconds.

    ◇ Walk around the perimeter of the room two times.

◇   Touch three walls in this room and then return to your seat.

◇   Touch your right elbow to your left knee and then your left elbow to your right knee. Do this ten times as fast as you can.

◇   Pat your head and rub your belly at the same time.

It is important to engage in the physical movement *with* your students. Your brain will benefit as well. For students who may not want to participate, explain why you're engaging in physical movement. You might say, "This is good for our brains. Let's see if we can pay better attention after this." Remember, also, to set a strict time limit, provide clear directions, and move immediately back into content afterward so you do not lose control of your class.

You might also consider providing students with a choice of activities so that everyone feels comfortable and that they can successfully participate. For example, while they discuss the content with their partners, you might allow students to choose between simply standing up or standing up while balancing on one foot. These desk-side physical-movement activities are short, fun, and highly engaging. (Seriously. They love it.)

Presenting Unusual or Intriguing Information

Because our brains seek novelty (Poldrack, 2011), incorporating unusual or intriguing information can be effective. Sharing such facts with students can attract their attention and help interest them in the topic at hand (Marzano, 2012). When something is unusual, our attention increases. I sometimes refer to this as the shiny object strategy. At the airport, for instance, my attention immediately went to the woman practicing yoga at the gate because this isn't something I normally see. She pulled my eye like a shiny object would.

You can find interesting facts online or often in your textbook's teacher edition. You can ask students to research and share intriguing information related to the current content. I also would like to offer you a list of resources that can help you gather information relevant to your content and students. Because such resources evolve so often, you can visit **go.SolutionTree.com/instruction** for live links.

Maintaining a Lively Pace

You know that if class moves too slowly, you can lose students to boredom. Conversely, if things move too quickly, you can lose them to frustration. Maintaining a lively pace that feels brisk but not hurried is a key way to ensure that students are with you for the entire period. Striking this balance gets easier over time. As you start, simply be aware of your pacing and when you feel like you're moving too quickly (versus times where the lesson seems to drag). By paying attention to how your students respond to a lesson, you'll gain clues as to how things are going. If students have their heads on their desks or seem to zone out, you might want to pick up the pace a bit. Conversely, if students seem flustered and are having trouble staying with you, you might want to slow down a tick.

It is important to diligently focus on pacing during this rejuvenation phase, especially as the weather gets nicer and the end of the school year is within sight. Students tend to become less focused when spring begins and they start anticipating summer break.

In terms of how to keep a lively pace, consider the following ideas (Marzano, 2012).

- **Use clear administrative tasks:** Ensure that you have clear procedures and routines for handing in assignments, distributing materials, and storing materials so you're not spending an inordinate amount of time on these routines. Review the procedures that you set up during the first anticipation phase to make sure they still work. If you are stuck here, seek advice from your mentor or veteran teachers in your building. They may have unique suggestions based on their years of experience.

- **Slow down when you present new content:** When you are presenting new content, allow students time to process the information both on their own and with others. They might talk with a partner or small group, or reflect on their own in writing. Use physical movement to break new content into digestible chunks so students are engaged in content for ten to fifteen minutes (elementary students) or twenty to thirty minutes (secondary students). Then take a brain break for three to five minutes before diving back into the content (Willis, 2016). Checking in with students via formative assessment strategies will help ensure that your pacing works for all students. Quick formative assessment strategies that reflect on your pacing include hand signals that allow students to self-assess their current topic understanding or collecting exit slips as students leave the classroom.

- **Employ seatwork:** Make sure your students know what to do if they finish an assignment early. This requires preparing independent activities that introduce students to another perspective on more advanced content, or that structure their study on a topic of their choice. They might also engage in sustained silent reading. The goal here isn't to have students do busywork, but to ensure they know exactly what to do related to academics when they have extra time, so they don't distract others, and you can keep pace.

- **Make smooth transitions:** Rules and procedures can help keep the pace lively but not too hurried as students move in and out of groups, to various activities, and to different stations. Practice transitions with students over and over again until they know exactly what you expect of them.

Have space on your board or wall for what you can call a parking lot. It can be a piece of chart paper or a designated spot on your whiteboard. If you or your students find yourselves stuck on a particular question or issue, write a note and put it in the parking lot. You can move on and revisit the topic at a later time after everyone has had time to think or gather information.

Self-Care Practices

First of all, celebrate again the fact that you've made it to the rejuvenation phase! Hopefully your self-care practices from previous phases helped get you to this place and you're using those that seem to work the best for you. I'm going to introduce two strategies that fit in nicely with this more positive phase of your first years of teaching. Developing a growth mindset (Dweck, 2006) and picturing your best possible future self will help you keep that positivity going strong.

Developing a Growth Mindset

In 2006, Carol S. Dweck introduced the world to growth versus fixed mindsets, and since then many teachers have been thinking about our students' mindsets and our own. We work hard to help our students establish growth mindsets so they don't believe that their intelligence is something they can't do anything about. We want them to know that persistence and hard work can mean academic growth. Don't forget to consider your mindset as a teacher. People with fixed mindsets believe that they cannot improve their practice and that they're the best they can be right now. If you have a growth mindset, you believe that you can definitely improve your practice, and that as you learn and work and reflect, you will continually get better and better at your craft.

Work to develop your growth mindset by being kind to yourself. Recognize that you're a beginner and it's OK to make mistakes. When you find yourself believing (or saying) that you can't do something, try adding the word *yet* to the end of that statement. Doing so can help you shift from a fixed mindset to a growth mindset. For example, rather than saying, "I'm not as good as my colleagues," change the statement to, "I'm not as good as my colleagues yet."

Try other ways to incorporate a growth mindset into your daily life.

- **Begin with awareness:** Notice when and where you're utilizing a fixed mindset so you can begin to change that.

- **Push through challenges:** Rather than quitting when things get tough, dig deep and keep going, picturing yourself having reached your goal. You did this to move through the disillusionment phase, and you can do it again whenever the going gets tough.

- **Seek constructive criticism:** Listen to people you trust and help them help you—particularly as you work to increase your abilities in the classroom.

- **Review your failures and mistakes:** You *will* have failures and mistakes, especially during your first years teaching. Accept this and think about what you can learn from these setbacks and how you can apply that learning to your own growth. By using this book, you'll be able to move forward from your failures and mistakes more easily.

- **Examine your words:** Be mindful of your own inner voice and ensure that you are speaking kindly to yourself. Talk to yourself the same way that you would talk to someone you love. Try addressing yourself in the third person instead of saying *I*. Research shows that using your name makes you more likely to give yourself advice and support (Starecheski, 2014).

- **Blast through the hard times:** Rather than shutting down when you feel discouraged, try working harder instead. Remember that your effort can change your outcome.

Picturing Your Best Possible Future Self

Research suggests that when you are optimistic about the future, you feel motivated to work toward that desired state, thus making that future more likely to become a reality (Sheldon & Lyubomirsky, 2006). Try this exercise to start picturing your future life as an educator (while keeping a growth mindset). By doing this, you can increase your current happiness and also pave the way for continued happiness in the future. I highly recommend writing out your responses here or in a different journal.

- Imagine your life in the future. What is the best possible life that you can imagine? Think of both your teaching and your personal life.

- For ten or fifteen minutes, write out your vision for the future. Be as specific as possible as you imagine yourself as an accomplished, expert teacher and successful in all other areas of your life as well. Where do you live? What does your classroom look like? How do you walk, talk, and act? How do you spend your free time? Who are you with?

- List the small steps that you can take now (and in the near future) to move toward your vision for the future.

By taking this time to envision your best possible future self, you are actually establishing what you want in your life, both professionally and personally. By thinking this way, you can start restructuring your priorities and commitments, which can move you toward this vision.

Reflections

Set aside time each day to reflect. The following prompts, related to classroom strategies and self-care practices for this phase in your first year, encourage this reflection. You don't need to respond to all of these in one sitting. Instead, dig into one or two at a time. Use the space at the end of this chapter to write about any other concerns or celebrations that you notice during the rejuvenation phase.

Classroom Strategy Prompts

Consider the following prompts in light of the rejuvenation phase.

- How do I show students that I truly love my job? What specific words and actions let students know how much I appreciate being with them? If there's an aspect of my day that I don't like, can I fake it until I make it?

- How often do students get to move in my classroom? Can I add one brain break tomorrow and consider whether it makes a difference? Do I notice a difference in student behavior on days when they move more?

- What shiny objects—unusual or intriguing information—do I present students? Where do I find interesting facts and ideas? Can my students help me find shiny objects that relate to our unit?

- How is my classroom pacing? Do things move along nicely? Are there slow or chaotic times? Have I checked my pacing by timing myself to see how long it takes to accomplish daily tasks? What administrative tasks can I make more efficient so I can slow down while presenting new content?

- What felt really good in my classroom? Why did it feel so good? How can I make this happen again?

Self-Care Practice Prompts

Consider the following prompts in light of the rejuvenation phase.

- Do I have a growth or fixed mindset when it comes to my classroom abilities? Can I recognize when I'm making a fixed-mindset statement? Have I tried adding *yet* to the end of such a statement?

- After completing the future self activity, what differences do I notice in my daily life? Can I truly picture myself as an expert teacher? Do I have more confidence and pride after completing that exercise? Am I comfortable sharing ideas with an administrator or my mentor, since he or she might help me reach my goals?

— NOTES —

CHAPTER 5

The Reflection Phase

You've been doing lots of reflecting during each phase, and here you are—at the reflection phase. Typically, you'll find yourself here around the end of the school year. This phase marks an incredibly exciting time. You're almost there! Can you believe it? Remember the anticipation phase? (See appendix A, on page 113, for end-of-the-year activity ideas.) Flip back to your first few entries and reread what you wrote so you can see how far you've come, how much better you know your students, how much growth everyone has made this year, and what you're looking forward to most next year. Consider what worked for you and your students this year—specifically. Why did it work? It's probably going to be difficult saying goodbye to these students, as you've no doubt formed some incredible relationships with them. Be gentle on yourself during this phase. You may be emotional. Because you may feel your feet firmly planted on the ground because you're more confident, allow yourself additional time to consider what is going well, what you might revise for next year, and what you want to let go of.

For this chapter's essay, I've decided to share one of my favorite lessons with you. I wrote it during my fourth year in the classroom and presented it to my students during that year's reflection phase.

My Favorite Lesson

This is a letter I gave to my students this year. I was terrified to do it. After having them turn in their vocabulary tests, I asked them to pick up this handout and read it over while waiting for everyone else to finish their tests. Those were the only instructions I gave. I then sat back and waited for their reactions. I saw smiles as they read the line about *lubricate*, and I saw perplexed looks as they tried to figure out why I had written this letter and if I would test them on it.

Dear students,

It's 10:00 on a Tuesday night, and I'm thinking about you guys. I'm thinking about our days together and all the things that I want you to know. Day after day, you listen to me tell you to sit down, spit out your gum, pull up your pants, write in your planner, and remember to turn in your progress report. I ask you to learn twenty new vocabulary words every two weeks (and beg you to please not use lubricate *in the way that you'd like to), and I constantly test your knowledge of figurative language by asking you to identify what I just used when I said, "You're as loud as fireworks on the Fourth of July today." I make you read, read, read, read, and write, write, write, write. I grade your behavior and your ability to work in groups. I have you become interrogative sentences and say that you can only ask questions for fifteen minutes. I assign poems so you become William Carlos Williams and write about why "so much depends / upon" your curling iron or worn-out toothbrush. Each day that you walk into my classroom, I expect the world from you and keep pushing you until you get it. I may not say it enough, but each one of you gives the world to me each and every day, so I'm sitting here thinking of you at 10:00 on a Tuesday evening.*

I met someone at the gym today who asked me what I do for a living. When I told him that I was a seventh-grade teacher, he immediately twisted up his face and asked, "Why?" Can you imagine? He actually asked me, "Why?" I told him, "Because I love it." And while that's true, I wanted so much to tell him everything that I was thinking. I was thinking that I do it because I love you guys. I love your age. I love that you flop into the classroom one day and never open your mouth and then the

*very next day, you leap back in and never shut your mouth. I love
that at the beginning of the school year you sit alone at your desk,
feeling that you'll never find another friend because this stupid
school put all of your friends on another team, and then three
months later I have to separate you from your six new best friends
because you can't stay on task when you're together. I love that
when we started the poetry unit, you groaned at me and rolled
your eyes, and a month later you asked me if you could write a
poem for your book review assignment. I love that you've joined
the football team or the cheerleading squad or the German club.
I love watching you grow taller than me in a few short months.
I love that when you get an A on your paper, your face lights
up brighter than the sun, and when you get a D you put your
head down and promise to try harder next time. And when you
do—although it may take more than one attempt, you usually
do—then you make my year.*

*I chose to teach middle school because you're the most fragile
age there is. At this time in your lives, you're forming your
adult personalities, and I'm so lucky to be a part of that. I'm so
lucky to see you every day and throw rules at you because those
rules will make you better people. So many adults are scared of
you guys. Terrified, in fact. You may not know it yet, but you
are scary, scary beings at this age. You're scary because you're so
unpredictable. Just when I think I've got you figured out, you go
and do something so out of the blue that I'm floored. And that's
why you're not scary to me—you're precious. You're growing into
adults right before my lucky eyes.*

*When I go home at night, I go home to an empty apartment.
I have no children of my own. But I am fulfilled. Fulfilled
because in actuality, I have 120 squirrelly children. I spend the
majority of each day with all of you and you fill me up. I have
gone through three major crises this year that could have shut
me down completely. Instead, I got up each day and came to you
guys because I knew that you would keep me going. When I walk
into the classroom and see you acting out Gardner's 1941 "The
Dinner Party" and yelling out the elements of the plot chart as
you perform, I am healed. When I see you giggling and acting
and learning, I know that I am in the right place. I push back*

my own personal struggles until I get home at night because I don't want to miss a single minute with you.

In the grand scheme of your life, you and I will share but only a moment. It is my hope that this moment that we're in will make a difference in your lives. I hope that you take your secret love of poetry or your knowledge of Harry Potter or your journal with you as you move above and beyond room 134 and do something magical with your life. Each and every one of you is a miracle, and I am blessed to be a part of you. You are the fourth group of students to come into my world, and I will not forget a single one of you. As I sit here thinking of you on this Tuesday night, I am smiling.

Thank you.

When they were done reading this letter, my students sort of looked up at me and smiled. Imagine that—I shared an individual smile with seventh graders through writing. A few students came up and asked if I wanted the letter back and when I told them it was a gift, they smiled again. I watched as they opened their folders and carefully put the purple sheet in a safe spot (just as I wished they'd do with every handout).

When everyone had finished reading, I stood at the front of the classroom (feeling totally exposed and vulnerable) and waited for responses.

One student asked, "You live in an apartment?" At first I felt irritated by that response—here I had poured my heart out to these children, and that's what Andy got out of it.

But then I realized he had picked out that detail because I had shared something personal with him. He liked that detail.

And so I told him, "Yes, I live in an apartment, and it has the ugliest brown carpet you've ever seen."

The class laughed and more comments started rolling in. "Did you write this yourself?" "What gym do you work out at?" "Do we need to have our parents sign this?" And finally, "Thanks." "Yeah, thank you." Aah, a thank-you. Heaven.

I did not have my students write me back this time. The joke's on them, though, because I will. I'll do it because when students write letters, they find their voice. They'll also learn the format of a friendly letter and how to edit and revise it. I'll build a rapport with some of the quiet students who are more comfortable sharing things on paper than aloud. And that is what every teacher needs to survive in a classroom of squirrelly students—a connection. They'll be learning but won't even know it, and that's the best kind of learning there is.

Later in the day another teacher approached me and asked if I had written my students a letter. I couldn't quite tell where he was going with his question. When I said that I had, he wanted to know what it said. I explained that it was a thank-you note of sorts.

Colleague: Well, it must have been more than that because they were all talking about it today and showing it to other students in my class.

Me: Really? In a good way?

Colleague: Yup. Nice job. They're actually reading. Would you mind putting a copy in my mailbox sometime?

My cup runneth over.

Prompts

As you learn about strategies and practices in this chapter, consider the following questions.

How do I share with students about myself on a personal level?

How do I connect with my students, particularly those who are harder to reach?

Would I rather share by talking or writing? How can I use my preference to engage with students in new ways?

Classroom Strategies

Now you can focus on your pedagogy and reflect on what's working. Because the reflection phase tends to correlate with the end of the year, adding a few more engagement and relationship or high-expectations strategies can help keep students engaged until the very last day of school. Specifically, I recommend focusing on questioning strategies (including how to ask in-depth questions of all students) and demonstrating value and respect for all learners. Recording yourself for just fifteen minutes while you instruct the class can help you see how well you're implementing these strategies. Now work on making conscious decisions about how to change your relationships with struggling students in order to demonstrate value and respect for them. Additionally, I include some fun end-of-the-year activities that I've used myself and that you might consider implementing in your own classroom.

Employing Questioning Strategies

Because we often cue and ask students questions, we must make sure we do so in an engaging way that ensures their learning. Marzano (2007, 2017) reports that this strategy increases response rates and outlines several ways to ask questions.

- **Random names:** Utilize an app like Pick Me!, Random Name Picker, or Random Number Generator (or write students' names on popsicle sticks) to choose which students respond to which questions. This helps you avoid calling only on students who volunteer. (Keep them engaged by either putting the selected student's stick back in the jar or in a cup hidden within the jar. That way students don't think they're off the hook for future questions.) Don't be afraid to call on the same student more than once, too; this helps keep their attention.

- **Hand signals:** Ask all students to give a hand signal in response to a question. For example, ask everyone, "How well does this make sense to you?" They can give a thumbs-up if it does make sense, a thumbs-down if it doesn't, and a thumbs-sideways if it doesn't make complete sense. Additionally, students can use hand signals to respond to questions that have yes-or-no answers or agree-or-disagree responses.

- **Response cards:** Give students clear plastic covers (insert blank paper) or whiteboards with markers so everyone is responsible for responding to all questions. After asking a question, all students respond in writing and then hold up their answers. (I swear there's something magical about this strategy. I think it's the novelty of getting to use markers. Of course, you have to let them play for a bit because they'll be fired up about these materials. Don't fight it. Tell them they have thirty seconds to scribble, draw, and write whatever they want before you get down to business. They're typically pretty responsive to this.)

- **Response chaining:** Rather than asking a question and having one student reply to you, try response chaining. It gets more students involved in the discussion (like a volleyball game versus a tennis match). After one student responds, another student says whether he or she agrees with what the first student said and why. Call on a third student to respond to the second student, and so on. This keeps everyone on his or her toes and engaged as active listeners.

- **Paired response:** Ask students to respond in pairs or elbow partners before calling on a pair to answer to the whole class. This allows for greater participation and a chance for students to support one another's thinking before sharing with the whole group. You can also use triads for this method.

- **Choral response:** This is particularly helpful when learning new vocabulary words. In choral response, the class repeats an answer as a whole group in order to imprint important information in students' minds.

- **Wait time:** Pause for at least three seconds after posing a question. This wait time, or think time, results in more student responses and more correct responses, and teacher questioning strategies "tend to be more varied and flexible" (Stahl, 1994). Additionally, pause if a student stops speaking in the middle of answering and after he or she has responded. This allows additional thinking and further responses. Mentally count to three. Our estimation abilities are not great; teachers usually wait less than one-and-a-half seconds (Fredericks, 2005; Stahl, 1994).

Under the same umbrella as these questioning strategies, make sure you're asking in-depth questions of all your students, not just the ones who beg to respond. This demonstrates that your classroom culture is one of high expectations for *all* students and that even your reluctant learners know that you believe in them. Teachers often overlook reluctant learners during discussions because a few students tend to dominate the discussions. In fact, research shows that teachers respond to engaged students in ways that further engagement; teachers behave differently toward students who aren't engaged in ways that undermine success and engagement (Reyes, Brackett, Rivers, White, & Salovey, 2012; Skinner & Belmont, 1993).

You can engage in supportive behaviors to help all students—even reticent ones—feel comfortable answering questions in class, particularly in-depth questions that may push students out of their comfort zone. Marzano (2007) provides multiple ways to do this.

- Demonstrate gratitude for all students' responses by thanking them (either publicly or privately).

- Do not allow negative comments from other students. Establish and enforce rules about being respectful when responding to others.

- Point out what is correct and what is incorrect in students' responses. Listen carefully when a student responds so you can point out what is working in the answer and what is not. This demonstrates that you appreciate when students take risks and that making mistakes is a natural part of the learning process.

- Restate the question or find a simpler one within it. This works as a form of scaffolding.

- Provide ways to temporarily let students off the hook. If a student is becoming frustrated, say, "What if you think about this and we'll come back to you in a bit?" When you do return to the student, you can ask the question the same way or in a different way. At that point, he or she has had time to gather thoughts and hear from other students.

Demonstrating Value and Respect for All Learners

You won't necessarily have a strong relationship with every single one of your students. There may be reluctant learners who hold back in class, not volunteering, being subdued, and preferring to work alone. First, recognize who these learners are; then reflect on how you might be treating these students differently than eager or extroverted students. For example, perhaps you rarely engage in playful dialogue with them.

Now make conscious decisions about how to change your relationships so you can demonstrate the value and respect you have for more introverted students. You can engage in the following behaviors to get started (Marzano, 2007).

- Frequently make eye contact with them.

- Smile at them at appropriate times. Maybe even give them a wink or a quick thumbs-up if this is your style.

- On occasion, make appropriate physical contact, such as putting a hand on the student's shoulder or giving a high five or fist bump if you know that a student's background and culture are OK with this. (If you're unsure, simply ask a student if it's OK before reaching out to him or her.)

- Maintain close proximity to them so you communicate interest (but not so close that you violate personal space).

- When appropriate, engage in playful dialogue with the identified students.

Gauge their reactions. Not all of these behaviors will be equally effective for your identified students, so it's important to reflect on how each strategy is working in order to support all of your students in important and powerful ways.

Self-Care Practices

Exactly as the name suggests, you are likely to feel much calmer and centered in the reflection phase. Like the rejuvenation phase, this phase is typically a positive one. The following strategies will help to add to this positivity: being inspired, writing yourself permission slips, setting aside time to reflect, and reflecting with someone else. As always, you don't need to implement every strategy. Instead, consider which appeals to you the most and start there.

Being Inspired

As you purposefully reflect on where you've been and where you're going, it can be beneficial to work on ways that you will stay *inspired* as an educator. Inspiration doesn't just hit. You can drum up some in the following ways.

- **Inspiration folder:** Start a single folder in which you collect positive notes from students, colleagues, parents, and administrators. You could also include inspirational quotes or images. Revisit this folder when you need a reminder of the good, important work you're doing. Another option is to turn this book or your reflection journal into a hybrid by including these quotes, images, and notes there rather than in a separate folder.

- **Inspirational movies:** Movies can inspire you. Classic examples include *Dead Poets Society*, *Freedom Writers*, *Good Will Hunting*, *Lean on Me*, *Mr. Holland's Opus*, and *Stand and Deliver*. I know that many Hollywood movies get a lot of things wrong about the teaching life, but there's usually a lesson worth taking away about relationships, patience, or perseverance.

- **Inspirational quotations:** Some people have said things really aptly, and sometimes their words help us remember to push through or celebrate. You could sign up for a quote-a-day email service so you can ruminate about one positive message per day. You might read this email around the time you're setting your daily intention. BrainyQuote (www.brainyquote.com) offers daily quote signup, and it and The Quote Garden (www.quotegarden .com) let you search by subject. Some of my favorite quotes follow. (Those from BrainyQuote have an asterisk).

  - "The important thing is not to stop questioning." —Albert Einstein*

  - "A teacher affects eternity; he can never tell where his influence stops." —Henry Adams*

  - "Education consists mainly of what we have unlearned." —Mark Twain*

  - "They may forget what you said, but they will never forget how you made them feel." —Carl Buehner (Evans, 1971)

  - "There are no mistakes or failures, only lessons." —Denis Waitley*

  - "You never lose until you quit trying." —Mike Ditka ("Positive," n.d.)

What are some of your favorites? List yours here.

- _____

  _____

Seek out stories that will help keep you inspired. *Chicken Soup for the Teacher's Soul* (Canfield & Hansen, 2012) is an example of a book that compiles short stories and quick anecdotes about being a teacher. You can visit **go.SolutionTree.com/instruction** to find other sources of inspirational quotes and stories for teachers.

Writing Yourself Permission Slips

Similar to setting an intention (as I described in the survival phase), I invite you to write a permission slip for yourself each day so that you feel inspired to take on your day in a positive way (Brown, 2015). In *Rising Strong*, Brené Brown (2015) describes writing her first permission slip on a sticky note before she was scheduled to meet Oprah Winfrey; the note said, "Permission to be excited, have fun, and be goofy" (p. 68). I love that! Rather than trying to stay calm and collected, Brown chose to give herself permission to fully experience this incredible moment.

By writing yourself a permission slip, you are allowing yourself to feel emotion. This is essential because your emotions may especially surprise you toward the end of the school year. You can think of giving yourself permission as an intention to stay aware. I write myself a permission slip prior to my workshops with educators and they often include the following statements.

- Recognize—and feel giddy about—this opportunity to work with amazing educators.
- Gather feedback and sort that feedback out for myself.
- Trust that I've done the necessary work.
- Be fully present and acknowledge the gift of learning today.
- Laugh and have fun today!

Consider granting yourself permission to do the following.

- Laugh at myself.
- Ask for help.
- Try new strategies in my classroom, even if I'm not sure they're going to work (at least the first few times).
- Take an uninterrupted lunch break.
- Take a ten-minute mindful walk during my plan period in order to breathe and relax.

- ◆ Reach out to a colleague to build a new relationship or ask for support.
- ◆ Go for a run after school rather than staying late to work.

By being intentional about your day, you can help ensure that you feel inspired, rather than defeated, at the end of the day.

Setting Aside Time to Reflect

You've been working to maintain your self-care practices throughout the easier and tougher parts of your first year. Now you're going to kick that up a notch and engage in purposeful reflection.

- ◆ **Ten extra minutes:** If you haven't done this already, try getting up just a few minutes earlier so you'll have uninterrupted time to reflect, set an intention, or engage in a mindfulness practice as you approach the chaotic end of the school year. What legacy do you want to leave and how can you manifest this during your final days of the year?

- ◆ **Journaling:** If you haven't had time to write in this book or another journal, make time *now* to record your reflections. Don't keep everything in your head. Writing these thoughts makes you more likely to recall your thinking and learn for next year (and the next year after that). Additionally, you'll be able to watch your progress and growth as a teacher by keeping track of how your reflections change from year to year.

Reflecting With Someone Else

Now is a good time to make sure that you are reflecting with another person as well as by yourself. Talking through your experiences, what you've felt and learned, and your goals and celebrations is an important ritual for your first few years of teaching (and throughout your entire teaching career). Talk about these with your mentor, coach, principal, a trusted colleague, friends, or family members so that you can fully articulate all you've experienced this year. Verbalizing our feelings also helps us self-regulate our emotions (Wolpert, 2007).

Reflections

Set aside time each day to reflect. The following prompts, related to classroom strategies and self-care practices for this phase in your first year, encourage this reflection. You don't need to respond to all of these in one sitting. Instead, dig into one or two at a time. Use the space at the end of this chapter to write about any other concerns or celebrations that you notice during the reflection phase.

Classroom Strategy Prompts

Consider the following prompts in light of the reflection phase.

- After watching a recording of myself during fifteen minutes of instruction, how many students did I call on? What was my wait time? Did I use any of the practices listed in this chapter—hand signals, whiteboards, and response chaining, for example?

- As I watch my questioning recording, is it clear that I expect all students to participate to the same degree? How do I follow up with different students? How complex are the questions I ask students? Do certain students answer only certain types or levels of questions? What expectations do my questioning skills demonstrate?

- How do I ensure that I'm reaching out to all students, particularly those who tend to be quieter or more reluctant? After reviewing my recording again, what verbal and nonverbal messages do I see myself sending to all students? Do I treat certain students differently? What might I do differently tomorrow in light of this evidence?

Self-Care Practice Prompts

Consider the following prompts in light of the reflection phase.

- Where do I turn for inspiration? Do I have a place in my journal or elsewhere to keep things that inspire me?

- What do I give myself permission to do—or not do? (Check the permission slip at the day's end to see if it stuck and if you noticed a difference.)

- When do I typically reflect? During my morning shower? On the drive to or from school? Can I formalize these natural reflection times by writing or recording my verbal thoughts to make my reflection more purposeful?

- Who do I trust enough to reflect with in person? Is there someone with whom I can schedule time to talk? (Share your intentions for the conversation beforehand and offer to also be a listening ear. Consider crafting questions ahead of time or using the prompts in this book to focus the conversation.)

– NOTES –

CHAPTER 6

The Second Anticipation Phase

A ah, summer. Glorious, beautiful summer has finally arrived. This time of year is all about you (and perhaps your partner, children, family, and friends outside school). During the second anticipation phase, after you've had time to fully recover from the school year and catch your breath, you will begin thinking ahead to the next school year. You're experiencing anticipation once again and feel excited about a fresh start next year. Each year brings to you new celebrations and challenges, but *you* bring increased expertise to your classroom.

As for this final essay, here are my thoughts on those beautiful summer days.

The Lazy Days of Summer

It's July 10. My cheeks are sun kissed, I'm watching the after-news rerun that normally signifies it's way past my bedtime, and I'm not planning on setting my alarm. No, I'm just going to get up when I get up, grab my bike, and hit the trail. I feel good. It's summer. Whether we'll openly admit it or not, summer is certainly one of the top selling points for our profession. This is time for you. You, you, and more you. This is your time to find your green thumb or your new muscles or that additional job that may allow you to buy that new tech toy you've had your eye on. At the very least, hit that snooze button. Twice, if you can.

By about the second or third week of freedom, you'll look in the mirror and realize that the bags under your eyes have disappeared, your hand gets tired just writing out a grocery list, and you're not quite sure what day of the week it is. Wow. You'll be sitting by the public pool listening to the children playing and you'll smile, knowing that you can keep reading your book because today those children are not your responsibility.

Or you'll be painting a house for a client who brings you lemonade. Or you will be pet-sitting the neighbors' dogs or working the cash register in the express lane at the corner store. You may even be in your classroom, teaching summer school for a week or two. Yes, you'll be working, but it will feel different in the summer. Even in the classroom, the mood changes when the sun is on the windows and you get to and from school by bike. The pressure is off in a way that you can hardly describe in words. Summer is magical this way. The change in your schedule and the change in your environment, scenery, and mind make the heat of the day feel like a refreshing breeze.

I recommend taking a vacation if you can—at least get in the car on a Tuesday and stay away until Thursday. Go to the grocery store in the middle of the afternoon and leisurely pick out your watermelon now that you have time. Clean out a closet or two. Have a garage sale and use the cash to buy yourself a treat you've had your eye on.

Enjoy your time off when you can, even if you're working another job. You deserve it. You've worked hard this year— harder than you imagined—and it's time to pamper yourself for longer than a three-day weekend. Give yourself one or two (or more) solid weeks of time before or after your summer job if you can. Read a brainless magazine; turn on a daytime talk show if you'd like. Just do your own thing.

When you become antsy and the school supplies arrive at the discount stores (Eeeeeeeee!), the upcoming school year will creep back into your mind. Now that there's space between you and the last school year, sit in the sun with your journal for an afternoon while you reflect and jot down notes. Think about how to make your life easier in the coming year. If something worked, figure out how you'll use it again. If you'd like to try something new (including a new self-care practice), take a few notes on how you'll do that but don't attempt a minute-by-minute lesson plan. When you run across a lesson that didn't work (and you may have quite a few of these; remember the growth mindset), find the humor in the attempt and decide how to improve it.

Unfortunately, in this career, you're unlikely to hit the point where you look back over the year and feel confident announcing, "That was a perfect year. Next year I'll do things exactly the same way. Ta-da!" Even if you do have yourself one terrific year—and you will—it won't repeat exactly the same way. You change; your students change. Heck, your students change from one class period to the next, even if they're all labeled the same age and ability group.

Don't spend your entire summer agonizing over the mistakes you may have made. Don't set up your entire lesson plan book so that you can pinpoint exactly what you'll be doing on December 16. This will backfire for sure.

However, there's one caveat: I do recommend thinking through and setting up your first week. The entire thing. Minute by minute. Decide how you'll do introductions, how you'll arrange the seats, how you'll organize supplies, and what you want to accomplish during the first five days. Your memory may be blurred at this point, but the first week is chaos. Remember? Students are changing classes, parents are in your face, you're attempting to memorize a bazillion new names—the less planning you have to do *during* the first week, the better. Go in one day early and make your copies so that you're not one of the sweating, swearing teachers kicking the copy machine two minutes before class is supposed to start. Your plans will change, just like always, but it's easier to change rather than to create plans when you have ninety-nine other things scrambling your brain.

It won't take you too long to do this, and you'll be much better at it once you've relaxed. For a little while, vow to do nothing remotely school related. Don't feel guilty. You likely spend nearly every minute of every day with school on your mind, so as much effort as it requires to stop that, stop that. Get back to you.

Aah, the lazy days of summer. Run through a sprinkler, lick an ice cream cone, applaud the fireworks, and forget about your lesson plan for a while.

Prompts

As you learn about strategies and practices in this chapter, consider the following questions.

What am I most looking forward to this summer?

What's one of my favorite summer memories from childhood? How can I reenact that memory this summer?

What can ease my transition between summer and the new school year?

Classroom Strategies

As you begin looking ahead to the next year or two, revisit the strategies you need more practice with. Once you feel confident with them, I recommend moving to the following resources to support your continued development of your own expertise as a classroom teacher: *Becoming a Reflective Teacher* (Marzano, 2012), *The Marzano Compendium of Instructional Strategies* (Marzano Resources, n.d.), and *The New Art and Science of Teaching* (Marzano, 2017). These resources will help you engage in continued deliberate practice around content-specific strategies. Many strategies apply in many circumstances. For example, you'll learn which ones work best when you're introducing brand-new content to students versus which ones work best when students are applying their knowledge. As you read more about teaching, try new lesson formats and strategies, and continue reflecting; your teaching skills and student experiences will continue improving.

Additionally, consider the following strategies to prepare for the upcoming school year.

- Decide how you want to arrange your classroom for next year. Consider how you might alter the physical layout based on how this school year went. Now that you've had time to adjust to your professional space, think about what worked for you and what didn't.

  ◇ Do you want to organize your supplies a different way?

  ◇ What supplies do you need to replenish or toss out?

  ◇ What new displays do you want to hang?

  ◇ What can you clean out of your desk to make space for the new year?

- Now that you have a bit of time, consider creating charts, game templates, and posters that you may not have had time to create during the school year. If you have any student exemplars from this year's projects or papers, consider adding those to your files (either hard copy or a photograph) so everything you need next year is in one place. If you can, laminate your materials to ensure that they last longer.

Self-Care Practices

As you move into the summer break and have more time to yourself, re-establish your self-care practices and revisit any strategies that you didn't have a chance to implement during the school year. As a final recommendation, I want to highlight some ways to have fun and act like a kid again.

Having Fun

You can have fun in lots of different ways, but here are some ideas.

- **Choose a theme song:** What song captures how you want to feel or puts you in a certain mood? Music can be a powerful way to increase our energy, put us in a good mood, or help to quiet our occupied minds. While you have a bit of extra time in the summer, consider creating playlists that will help set your mood during the upcoming school year.

- **Learn something new:** Pick up a new hobby or sport or take a class and use your newly developed growth mindset and optimism to engage your brain in a new way. Take a lesson to learn how to play tennis or knit or dance. Be the student!

- **Read:** Now that you have a bit more time, indulge in reading for pleasure or your own professional development. Spend an afternoon exploring new sections of the local bookstore or library and see what appeals to you.

- **Tour your own city:** Become a tourist in your own city. Take yourself on a field trip to the museums, restaurants, or galleries that you haven't visited before.

- **Forget the alarm:** Enjoy the true pleasure of not having to live by an alarm if you can. Sleep until you naturally wake up and see what it feels like to enter your day refreshed and fully rejuvenated.

- **Go to an event:** Splurge on a concert, game, lecture, or event that you might not have time for during the school year. Is it out of town but near enough for an overnight? Book a hotel room.

- **Get active:** Walk, hike, bike, run, compete in a triathlon—anything to get your blood pumping and your heart beating strong!

- **Spend time outside:** Go fishing, play a few rounds of golf, or take a blanket to the park, take your shoes off, and feel the sun on your face.

Acting Like a Kid Again

Teaching can force us to grow up immediately. To honor our younger selves, it can be extremely rejuvenating and fun to engage in the activities that we loved as kids. Kids have fun—they run, skip, and dance in carefree ways. Play makes us happy (Shute, 2009), so consider ways that you can have some fun this summer. You might run through a sprinkler, visit an amusement park, buy a treat from the ice cream truck, catch fireflies, blow bubbles, light sparklers, have a dance party in your kitchen, hula hoop, build a sandcastle, or have a picnic in the park. Enjoy anything that reminds you of your carefree summer days as a student.

Reflections

Set aside time to reflect, even in the summer. The following prompts, related to classroom strategies and self-care practices for this phase in your first year, encourage this reflection. You don't need to respond to all of these in one sitting. Instead, dig into one or two at a time. Use the space at the end of this chapter to write about any other concerns or celebrations that you notice during the second anticipation phase.

Classroom Strategy Prompts

Consider the following prompts in light of the second anticipation phase.

- Do I look forward to returning to teaching next year? What areas of my classroom bring me joy? What areas of my room frustrate me and how can I address those frustrations? Does my classroom feel inviting and refreshed for next year's students?

- What projects can I complete this summer that I didn't have time for during the school year? Are there any games or posters that I can create, cut out, organize, or laminate? Do I have any student exemplars that I want to hold onto? What will I wish I had done over the summer as the next school year starts?

Self-Care Practice Prompts

Consider the following prompts in light of the second anticipation phase.

- ◆ What are my favorite things to do for fun? How can I plan for and ensure that I make time for fun this summer? Who might I invite to join me?

- ◆ What did I love to do as a child that as an adult I haven't had time to do? How can I revisit some of the things that I used to love now that I have some time to play?

— NOTES —

The Year
in Retrospect

It has truly been my sincere pleasure and honor to be by your side as you maneuvered through your first year (or two or three) in the classroom. I applaud your efforts and dedication to not only your content, but to your students. I am in awe of you. Because the world of education in general is so challenging, I am humbled by teachers' quiet dedication and determination—particularly our newest educators. I offer my sincere gratitude to you for choosing this profession and for sticking with it, even when you wondered how you would make it to the end of the day. I will continue cheering you on, from afar, as you increase your expertise and continue changing students' lives.

Be proud of what you've accomplished this year. You navigated this challenging year's various phases while keeping an eye on the essential classroom strategies and self-care practices that had the biggest impact on your students and on you. You may have formed relationships with your students that will last a lifetime. I'm willing to bet that you celebrated your students' growth, kept them engaged, and greeted them at the classroom door each and every day. You reflected on your work, thoughts, and goals, and now you have a pretty incredible resource that documents your first years as a classroom teacher. You will cherish looking back on this documentation of your life. You might even pass this gift to your own student teacher someday.

As you continue developing your expertise around various class-room strategies, I strongly encourage you to remember the power of your self-care practices. Recall how you feel when you get a good night's sleep. Notice how healthy food choices boost your energy level. Continue being grateful for your amazing career, and grant yourself permission to make each day full of awesome.

I now present to you the same questions that you answered in the introduction. Before you look back at your initial responses, answer them here (or in your journal). Then look back to see if or how you've changed over this year.

Who or what inspires you and why?

_____

_____

_____

_____

_____

What was school like for you? What would you like to change about your own childhood experience and young adult experience in school?

_____

_____

_____

_____

_____

How do you learn best? How does your best friend
learn best? Why is it important to recognize that we
learn differently?

_____

_____

_____

_____

_____

Why did you choose this noble profession above all the
other careers available to you?

_____

_____

_____

_____

_____

What is your greatest hope for your first year? Your
fifth year? Your twenty-fifth year?

_____

_____

_____

_____

_____

What fuels you? In other words, what gives you energy?

_____

_____

_____

_____

_____

What does self-care look like for you?

_____

_____

_____

_____

_____

I am so proud of you and grateful for you. Continue to shine and grow! Good luck. You've got this! You've so got this.

End-of-the-Year Activities

Because the end of the school year is unlike any other time of the year, I've included an appendix for you with some of my favorite end-of-the-year activities that worked particularly well for me and for my students. As you read through these ideas, consider how you might modify them to meet your own needs based on the students you teach.

Inviting and Disinviting Feedback

As the school year winds down, consider seeking feedback from your students. It can help you reflect on your first year and prepare for your second year (and third, and so on). One way to get feedback is by asking students to respond in the ways I present in figure A.1 (page 114).

Explain the terms *inviting* and *disinviting* to your students and ask them to list specific things for each. For younger students, you might alter the prompt to read *This felt good or welcoming* and *This didn't feel good or welcoming*. Ideally, students do this anonymously so that you get the most honest responses. You may need to do this orally with elementary students and word the prompt so that it makes sense to them. You might also think about asking your students' parents or guardians to respond to these same prompts.

This felt inviting	This felt disinviting

Source: Adapted from Purkey, 1978.

Figure A.1: Ask students for feedback.

*Visit **go.SolutionTree.com/instruction** for a free reproducible version of this figure.*

Students often list the following things as inviting.

- When we have a choice in what activity we get to do
- When we play games
- When you ask us about our weekends
- When you tell us that you're proud of us
- When we get to move around the classroom
- When we take brain breaks in class

These behaviors often come up under uninviting.

- When it takes forever to get our assignments back
- When we have to stay in our own seats all day
- When we have multiple tests in one day
- When the same students get recognized for their work every time
- When we can't have our cell phones in class
- When we don't have time to get started on our homework during class

End-of-the-Year Letters

If appropriate, ask each student to provide you with an end-of-the-year letter. You can supply students with sample prompts or simply ask them to write you letters, sharing their personal reflections on the entire school year. Elementary students might do this orally or in a drawing. These prompts can help students get started, and you can visit **go.SolutionTree.com/instruction** for a free reproducible version of these questions.

- What was your favorite lesson, activity, or unit this year? Why?
- What are you proudest of this year?
- What was your biggest challenge this year?
- What are you most excited about for next year?
- What are your summer plans?

Survival Guides

I loved asking my students to create their own seventh-grade survival guide for the next year's students. I gave them prompts, and they selected half or so to include in their guides. They were able to be creative with this assignment by including pictures that they printed and drew. You could certainly have students do this electronically, too (with PowerPoint, for example). You can visit **go.SolutionTree.com/instruction** to access a free reproducible version of the prompts, which include the following.

- Study tips
- Best ways to organize their locker
- Clubs, sports, and activities that you recommend
- The top-five things they need to know about their teacher
- What they might be excited to learn about
- How they can deal with their parents
- Fashion tips
- The best classes at their school
- The best things about being at their school
- Free choice

Pay-It-Forward Promises

Pay-it-forward promises is another activity that I loved doing at the end of the school year. Hand students a note card and ask them to write down what they think about their future selves. How could they pay their inevitable success forward—either to the school or to me, personally? For example, if a student wants to be a famous author someday, he might pay it forward by promising to give five copies of his published book to the school (signed, of course). If another student wants to be a famous singer, she might pay it forward by promising two free front-row tickets to her sold-out show. Students loved this activity, and I still have my boxes of note cards, filled with promises and big dreams.

Reflections

To encourage even further reflection toward the end of the school year, use the space provided to write about any concerns you have noticed or celebrations you have made.

The following prompts will spur your thinking.

- What fun activities, toward the end of the school year, will encourage my students to reflect and celebrate?

- What are my top-three shining moments for this year? What am I proudest of? (Record your answers so you don't forget them, and don't be modest.)

- Which student showed the most growth? How does that make me feel? Why?

- What lessons did I learn this year?

- What advice would I give to a new teacher?

- Which part of the school day was my favorite? Why?

- What caused the most stress this year?

- What am I most looking forward to next year?

- Knowing what I now know, would I still choose teaching?

– NOTES –

— NOTES —

Mementos

Here is a space for you to paste mementos—notes from students, parents, administrators, and colleagues; newsletters or newspaper articles that explain events that occurred during the year; photographs of your first classroom, your first students, your first holiday gift, your first confiscated note between students, and the like. Placing these memories here, where you've written your reflections, will mean having everything in one place. Look back here on occasion to reflect on how much you've grown.

REFERENCES AND RESOURCES

Active listening. (n.d.). Accessed at www.skillsyouneed.com/ips/active-listening.html on December 5, 2017.

Adams, H. (2014). *The education of Henry Adams*. Seattle, WA: CreateSpace.

Aguilar, E. (2014, December 11). *Setting intentions: A powerful tool to help us learn* [Blog post]. Accessed at www.edutopia.org/blog/setting-intentions-powerful -tool-help-us-learn-elena-aguilar on April 29, 2017.

Allen, M. B. (2005). *Eight questions on teacher recruitment and retention: What does the research say?* Denver, CO: Education Commission of the States.

Anthony, G., & Kane, R. (2008). *Making a difference: The role of initial teacher education and induction in the preparation of secondary teachers*. Wellington, New Zealand: Teaching and Learning Research Initiative.

Berkeley Wellness—University of California. (n.d.). *14 keys to a healthy diet* [Slide show]. Accessed at www.berkeleywellness.com/healthy-eating/food/slideshow/14 -keys-to-a-healthy-diet on April 29, 2017.

Bloom, B. S. (Ed.). (1956). *Taxonomy of educational objectives: The classification of educational goals; Handbook I: Cognitive domain*. New York: David McKay.

Blue light has a dark side. (2015, September 2). Accessed at www.health.harvard.edu /staying-healthy/blue-light-has-a-dark-side on September 3, 2017.

Boogren, T. H. (2015). *Supporting beginning teachers*. Bloomington, IN: Marzano Resources.

Brady, A. (n.d.). *Mindful walking practice: How to get started*. Accessed at www.chopra .com/articles/mindful-walking-practice-how-to-get-started on April 29, 2017.

BrainyQuote. (n.d.). *Home*. Accessed at www.brainyquote.com on November 4, 2017.

Breaux, A. L., & Wong, H. K. (2003). *New teacher induction: How to train, support, and retain new teachers*. Mountain View, CA: Wong.

Brown, B. (n.d.) *Home*. Accessed at www.courageworks.com on December 5, 2017.

Brown, B. (2015). *Rising strong*. New York: Spiegel & Grau.

Calaprice, A. (2000). *The expanded quotable Einstein*. Princeton, NJ: Princeton University Press.

Canfield, J., & Hansen, M. V. (2012). *Chicken soup for the teacher's soul: Stories to open the hearts and rekindle the spirits of educators*. New York: Simon & Schuster.

Carpenter, D. (n.d.). *The science behind gratitude (and how it can change your life)*. Accessed at https://my.happify.com/hd/the-science-behind-gratitude on May 1, 2017.

Carson, J. W., Carson, K. M., Gil, K. M., & Baucom, D. H. (2004). Mindfulness-based relationship enhancement. *Behavior Therapy, 35*, 471–494.

Clotfelter, C. T., Ladd, H. F., & Vigdor, J. L. (2007). *Are teacher absences worth worrying about in the U.S.?* Accessed at www.nber.org/papers/w13648 on August 19, 2017.

Colvin, G. (2008). *Talent is overrated: What really separates world-class performers from everybody else*. New York: Portfolio.

Cook, G. (2013). Why we are wired to connect. *Scientific American*. Accessed at https://scientificamerican.com/article/why-we-are-wired-to-connect on April 29, 2017.

DeNoon, D. J. (2009, March 23). *7 rules for eating*. WebMD. Accessed at https://.webmd.com/food-recipes/news/20090323/7-rules-for-eating#1 on November 4, 2017.

Donnelly, J. E., & Lambourne, K. (2011). Classroom-based physical activity, cognition, and academic achievement. *Preventive Medicine, 52*(Supplement 1), S36–S42.

Dweck, C. S. (2006). *Mindset: The new psychology of success*. New York: Random House.

Ericcson, K. A. (2006). The influence of experience and deliberate practice on the development of superior expert performance. In K. A. Ericsson, N. Charness, P. J. Feltovich, & R. R. Hoffman (Eds.), *The Cambridge handbook of expertise and expert performance* (pp. 685–705). Cambridge, England: Cambridge University Press.

Ericsson, K. A., Krampe, R. T., & Tesch-Romer, C. (1993). The role of deliberate practice in the acquisition of expert performance. *Psychological Review, 100*(3), 363–406.

Evans, R. L. (1971). *Richard Evans' quote book*. Salt Lake City, UT: Publishers Press.

Feiman-Nemser, S. (2001). From preparation to practice: Designing a continuum to strengthen and sustain teaching. *Teacher's College Record, 103*(6), pp. 1013–1055.

Fredericks, A. D. (2005). *The complete idiot's guide to success as a teacher*. New York: Pearson.

Gardner, M. (1941, January 31). The dinner party. *The Saturday Review of Literature, 25*(5). Accessed at https://my.hrw.com/support/hos/hostpdf/host_text_103.pdf on December 6, 2017.

Gatens, B. P. (2014, May 22). *Avoiding toxic humor: Why there's no room for sarcasm in the classroom* [Blog post]. Accessed at https://education.cu-portland.edu/blog /curriculum-teaching-strategies/theres-no-room-for-sarcasm-in-the-classroom on December 5, 2017.

Gregoire, C. (2015). *What constant exposure to negative news is doing to our mental health*. Accessed at www.huffingtonpost.com/2015/02/19/violent-media -anxiety_n_6671732.html on September 3, 2017.

Grothaus, M. (2015, September 1). *How giving up refined sugars changed my brain*. Accessed at www.fastcompany.com/3050319/how-giving-up-refined-sugar -changed-my-brain on November 4, 2017.

Hanushek, E. A., Kain, J. F., & Rivkin, S. G. (1998). *Teachers, schools, and academic achievement* (Working paper no. 6691). Cambridge, MA: National Bureau of Economic Research.

Haynes, M. (2014, July 14). *On the path to equity: Improving the effectiveness of beginning teachers*. Alliance for Excellent Education. Accessed at https://all4ed .org/reports-factsheets/path-to-equity on November 3, 2017.

Hülsheger, U. R., Alberts, H. J. E. M., Feinholdt, A., & Lang, J. W. B. (2013). Benefits of mindfulness at work: The role of mindfulness in emotion regulation, emotional exhaustion, and job satisfaction. *Journal of Applied Psychology, 98*(2), 310–325.

Humphrey, T. (2003). *In the first few years: Reflections of a beginning teacher*. Newark, DE: International Reading Association.

Hyatt, M. (n.d.). *How to find a mentor to help you go further, faster*. Accessed at https://michaelhyatt.com/find-mentor.html on September 2, 2017.

Jensen, E. (2005). *Teaching with the brain in mind* (2nd ed.). Alexandria, VA: Association for Supervision and Curriculum Development.

Jonas, P. M. (2010). *Laughing and learning: An alternative to shut up and listen*. Lanham, MD: Rowman & Littlefield.

Kabat-Zinn, J. (1994). *Wherever you go, there you are.* New York: Hyperion.

Lin, J. (2009). *Mindfulness reduces stress, promotes resilience.* Accessed at https:// newsroom.ucla.edu/stories/using-mindfulness-to-reduce-stress-96966 on September 2, 2017.

Marzano Resources. (n.d.). *The Marzano Compendium of Instructional Strategies.* Accessed at www.marzanoresources.com/online-compendium/intro on July 19, 2017.

Marzano, R. J. (2007). *The art and science of teaching: A comprehensive framework for effective instruction.* Alexandria, VA: Association for Supervision and Curriculum Development.

Marzano, R. J. (2012). *Becoming a reflective teacher.* Bloomington, IN: Marzano Resources.

Marzano, R. J. (2017). *The new art and science of teaching.* Bloomington, IN: Solution Tree Press.

Marzano, R. J., & Pickering, D. J. (2011). *The highly engaged classroom.* Bloomington, IN: Marzano Resources.

Mayo Clinic Staff. (2016). *Exercise: 7 benefits of regular physical activity.* Accessed at https://mayoclinic.org/healthy-lifestyle/fitness/in-depth/exercise/art-20048389 on April 29, 2017.

McCaffrey, D. F., Lockwood, J. R., Koretz, D. M., & Hamilton, L. S. (2003). *Evaluating value-added models for teacher accountability.* Santa Monica, CA: RAND. Accessed at www.rand.org/pubs/monographs/2004/RAND_MG158 .pdf on July 19, 2017.

Miller, R. T., Murnane, R. J., & Willett, J. B. (2007). *Do teacher absences impact student achievement? Longitudinal evidence from one urban school district.* Accessed at www.nber.org/papers/w13356 on August 19, 2017.

Mohan, G. (2013, March 26). Social isolation increases risk of early death, study finds. *Los Angeles Times.* Accessed at https://articles.latimes.com/2013/mar/26 /science/la-sci-social-isolation-health-20130326 on July 19, 2017.

Moir, E. (2011, August). *Phases of first-year teaching* [Blog post]. Accessed at https:// newteachercenter.org/blog/2011/08/17/phases-of-first-year-teaching on October 18, 2017.

Moir, E., Barlin, D., Gless, J., & Miles, J. (2009). *New teacher mentoring: Hopes and promise for improving teacher effectiveness.* Cambridge, MA: Harvard Education Press.

National Sleep Foundation. (n.d.a). *Electronics in the bedroom: Why it's necessary to turn off before you tuck in.* Accessed at https://sleepfoundation.org/ask-the-expert /electronics-the-bedroom on April 29, 2017.

National Sleep Foundation. (n.d.b). *How much sleep do we really need?* Accessed at https://sleepfoundation.org/how-sleep-works/how-much-sleep-do-we-really-need on April 29, 2017.

Nye, B., Konstantopoulos, S., & Hedges, L. V. (2004). How large are teacher effects? *Educational Evaluation and Policy Analysis, 26*(3), 237–257.

Peri, C. (n.d.). *10 things to hate about sleep loss.* Accessed at https://webmd.com/sleep -disorders/features/10-results-sleep-loss on April 29, 2017.

Pianta, R. C., Hamre, B., & Stuhlman, M. (2003). Relationships between teachers and children. In Irving B. Weiner (Ed.), *Handbook of psychology* (pp. 199–234). Hoboken, NJ: Wiley.

Poldrack, R. (2011, November 17). *Multitasking: The brain seeks novelty* [Blog post]. Accessed at www.huffingtonpost.com/russell-poldrack/multitasking-the-brain -se_b_334674.html on April 29, 2017.

Pollan, M. (2009). *In defense of food.* London: Penguin.

Positive quotes for kids. (n.d.). Accessed at www.best-speech-topics.com/positive -quotes-for-kids.html on December 6, 2017.

Prueher, I. (2017, March 6). *Establish a sleep routine for your kids and yourself—Get the rest you need (part 3 in a 3-part series).* Accessed at www.huff.to/1MjLLRQ on April 29, 2017.

Public Education Network. (2003). *The voice of the new teacher.* Washington, DC: Author. Accessed at www.publiceducation.issuelab.org/resources/14442/14442 .pdf on July 19, 2017.

Purkey, W. W. (1978). *Inviting school success: A self-concept approach to teaching and learning.* Belmont, CA: Wadsworth.

Restonic. (2017, January 16). *Weekday sleep vs. weekend sleep* [Blog post]. Accessed at www.restonic.com/blog/weekday-sleep-weekend-sleep-2228 on April 29, 2017.

Reyes, M. R., Brackett, M. A., Rivers, S. E., White, M., & Salovey, P. (2012). Classroom emotional climate, student engagement, and academic achievement. *Journal of Educational Psychology, 104*(3), 700–712.

Roorda, D. L., Koomen, H. M. Y., Spilt, J. L., & Oort, F. J. (2011). The influence of affective teacher–student relationships on students' school engagement and achievement: A meta-analytic approach. *Review of Educational Research, 81*(4), 493–529.

Roskos, K., Vukelich, C., & Risko, V. (2001). Reflection and learning to teach reading: A critical review of literacy and general teacher education studies. *Journal of Literacy Research, 33*(4), 595–635.

Rowan, B., Correnti, R., & Miller, R. (2002). What large-scale survey research tells us about teacher effects on student achievement: Insights from the prospects study of elementary schools. *Teachers College Record, 104*(8), 1525–1567.

Russell, H. (n.d.). *How to start a gratitude practice to change your life* [Blog post]. Accessed at https://tinybuddha.com/blog/how-to-start-a-gratitude-practice-to-change-your-life on April 29, 2017.

Salleh, M. R. (2008, October). Life event, stress, and illness. *Malaysian Journal of Medical Sciences, 15*(4), 9–18.

Sanders, W. L., Wright, S. P., & Horn, S. P. (1997). Teachers and classroom context effects on student achievement: Implications for teacher evaluation. *Journal of Personnel Evaluation in Education, 11*(1), 57–67.

Selhub, E. (2015, November 17). *Nutritional psychiatry: Your brain on food* [Blog post]. Accessed at www.health.harvard.edu/blog/nutritional-psychiatry-your-brain-on-food-201511168626 on November 4, 2017.

Sheldon, K. M., & Lyubomirsky, S. (2006). How to increase and sustain positive emotion: The effects of expressing gratitude and visualizing best possible selves. *Journal of Positive Psychology, 1*(2), 73–82.

Shute, N. (2009, March 9). 10 reasons play can make you healthy, happy, and more productive. *U.S. News & World Report.* Accessed at https://health.usnews.com/health-news/family-health/childrens-health/articles/2009/03/09/10-reasons-play-can-make-you-healthy-happy-and-more-productive on December 6, 2017.

Skinner, B. F. (1948). "Superstition" in the pigeon. *Journal of Experimental Psychology, 38*(2), 168.

Skinner, E. A., & Belmont, M. J. (1993). Motivation in the classroom: Reciprocal effects of teacher behavior and student engagement across the school year. *Journal of Education Psychology, 85*(4), 571–581.

Sousa, D. A. (2017). *How the brain learns.* Thousand Oaks, CA: Corwin Press.

Southwick, S. M., & Charney, D. S. (2012). *Resilience: The science of mastering life's greatest challenges.* New York: Cambridge University Press.

Sparks, S. D. (2016, August 4). How feeling respected transforms a student's relationship to school. *PBS News Hour.* Accessed at www.pbs.org/newshour/education/feeling-respected-transforms-student-school on December 5, 2017.

Stahl, R. J. (1994). *Using "think-time" and "wait-time" skillfully in the classroom.* Accessed at https://ericdigests.org/1995-1/think.htm on September 3, 2017.

Stansbury, K., & Zimmerman, J. (2000). *Lifelines to the classroom: Designing support for beginning teachers.* San Francisco: WestEd.

Starecheski, L. (2014, October 7). *Why saying is believing—The science of self-talk*. Accessed at www.npr.org/sections/health-shots/2014/10/07/353292408/why -saying-is-believing-the-science-of-self-talk on September 3, 2017.

Tang, Y. Y., Ma, Y., Wang, J., Fan, Y., Feng, S., Lu, O., et al. (2007). Short-term meditation training improves attention and self-regulation. *Proceedings of the National Academy of Sciences of the United States of America, 104*(43), 17152–17156.

Twain, M. (2006). *Mark Twain's notebook*. A. Paine (Ed.). Hong Kong, China: Hesperides Press.

United States Department of Health and Human Services Office of Disease Prevention and Health Promotion. (n.d.). *2008 physical activity guidelines for Americans summary*. Accessed at https://health.gov/paguidelines/guidelines/summary.aspx on April 29, 2017.

United States Navy. (n.d.) *Combat tactical breathing*. Accessed at www.med.navy.mil /sites/nmcphc/Documents/health-promotion-wellness/psychological-emotional -wellbeing/Combat-Tactical-Breathing.pdf on August 19, 2017.

van Manen, M. (1995). *On the epistemology of reflective practice*. Accessed at www .maxvanmanen.com/on-the-epistemology-of-reflective-practice-2 on February 5, 2018.

Webb, N. L. (2002). *Depth-of-knowledge levels for four content areas*. Accessed at http://facstaff.wcer.wisc.edu/normw/All%20content%20areas%20%20DOK% 20levels%2032802.pdf on September 3, 2017.

Williams, W. C. (1938). *The collected poems of William Carlos Williams, volume I, 1909–1939*. C. MacGowan (Ed.). New York: New Directions.

Willis, J. (2016, December 7). Using brain breaks to restore students' focus. *Edutopia*. Accessed at www.edutopia.org/article/brain-breaks-restore-student -focus-judy-willis on February 1, 2018.

Winerman, L. (2005). *The mind's mirror*. Accessed at www.apa.org/monitor/oct05 /mirror.aspx on April 29, 2017.

Wolpert, S. (2007). *Putting feelings into words produces therapeutic effects in the brain; UCLA neuroimaging study supports ancient Buddhist teachings*. Accessed at https:// newsroom.ucla.edu/releases/Putting-Feelings-Into-Words-Produces-8047 on September 3, 2017.

INDEX

Supporting Beginning Teachers
Tina H. Boogren
Foreword by Robert J. Marzano
Give new teachers the time and professional guidance they need to become expert teachers through effective mentoring. Investigate key research, and examine the four types of support—physical, emotional, instructional, and institutional—that are crucial during a teacher's first year in the classroom.
BKL023

Motivating and Inspiring Students
Robert J. Marzano, Darrell Scott, Tina H. Boogren, and Ming Lee Newcomb
Bringing motivation and inspiration to the classroom is not easy. With this practical resource, you'll discover a results-driven framework—based on a six-level hierarchy of student needs and goals—that you can use to provide engaging instruction to students.
BKL025

Becoming a Reflective Teacher
Robert J. Marzano
Learn how to combine a model of effective instruction with goal setting, focused practice, focused feedback, and observations to improve your instructional practices. Included are 280 strategies related to the 41 elements of effective teaching shown to enhance student achievement.
BKL011

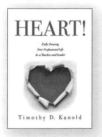

HEART!
Timothy D. Kanold
Explore the concept of a heartprint—the distinctive impression an educator's heart leaves on students and colleagues during his or her professional career. Use this resource to reflect on your professional journey and discover how to foster productive, heart-centered classrooms and schools.
BKF749

Wait! Your professional development journey doesn't have to end with the last pages of this book.

We realize improving student learning doesn't happen overnight. And your school or district shouldn't be left to puzzle out all the details of this process alone.

No matter where you are on the journey, we're committed to helping you get to the next stage.

Take advantage of everything from **custom workshops** to **keynote presentations** and **interactive web and video conferencing**. We can even help you develop an action plan tailored to fit your specific needs.

Let's get the conversation started.

Call 888.763.9045 today.